THE WARRIOR'S PATH

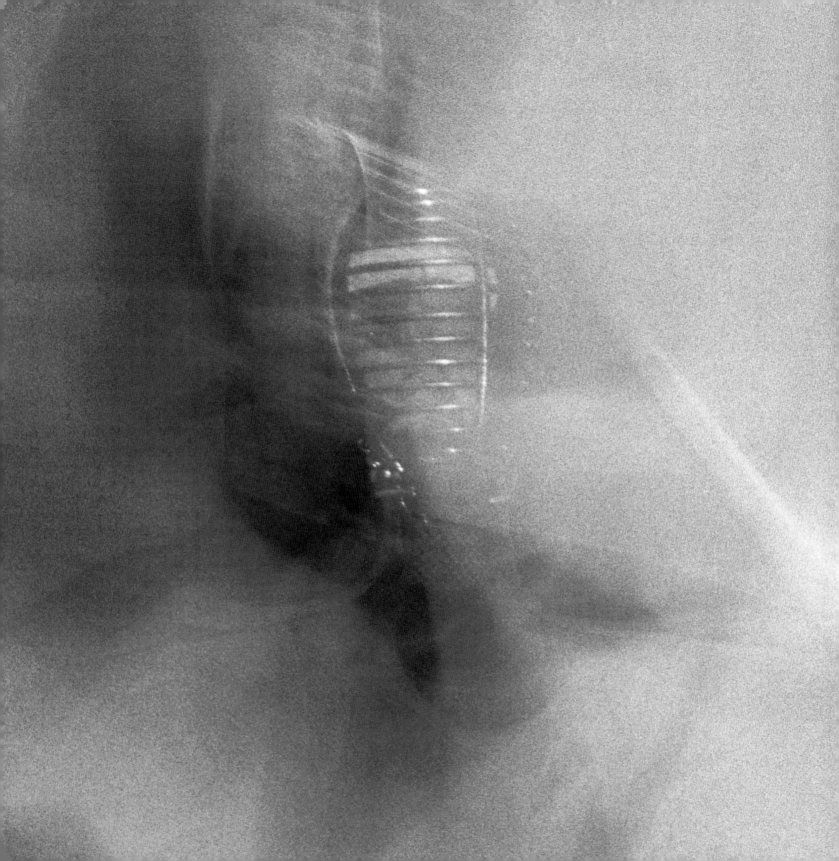

The
WARRIOR'S PATH

Wisdom from Contemporary
Martial Arts Masters

James Sidney

Shambhala · BOSTON · 2003

Shambhala Publications, Inc.
Horticultural Hall
300 Massachusetts Avenue
Boston, Massachusetts 02115
www.shambhala.com

9 8 7 6 5 4 3 2 1

First Shambhala Edition
Printed in Singapore
Designed by Peter Maher

♾ This edition is printed on acid-free paper that meets the
American National Standards Institute Z39.48 Standard.

Distributed in the United States by Random House, Inc.

Library of Congress Cataloging-in-Publication Data
The warrior's path: wisdom from contemporary martial arts masters /
edited by James Sidney.—1st Shambhala ed.
p. cm.
ISBN 1-59030-074-2 (pbk.: alk. paper)
1. Martial arts—Japan. 2. Martial artists. I. Sidney, James, 1972–
GV1100.77.A2W37 2003
796.8—dc21
2003006776

Contents

For my teacher, Masami Tsuruoka, who inspired me to meet the fourteen other extraordinary men and women of this volume.

It is my great privilege to celebrate the spirit and careers of the fifteen masters of this book. My deepest thanks is owed to them for sharing their time, ideas and, in many instances, their homes with me.

I am indebted also to dozens of other individuals who assisted with the research, logistics, interviews or photography. Among those who gave advice and assistance I would like to thank Hiroshi Nakamura sensei, Dr. David B. Waterhouse and Kim A. Taylor sensei. I am also grateful for the translating efforts of Kiyokazu Endo and Mari Endo, the hospitality and friendship of Hardy and Judi Dawainis, the hospitality of Savana Burke and Rebecca Greco, and in particular, the support and confidence of Dennis and Diane Stewart.

Several assistants or family members of the masters were also instrumental in this book's creation. I would like to extend my sincere thanks to Ari Kurose kyoshi, Dr. Shelley Fernandez, Kosaku Tanaka sensei, Kozo Awazu, Tony Lima, Steve Hope, June Takahashi, and especially to Koya Shishime of the All Japan Kyudo Federation, for his extraordinary kindness and generosity.

Special thanks is also due to my interpreter in Tokyo, Akiyo Yamane, for her untiring efforts both during and after my visits to Japan.

The many talents of Andrew Bowerbank are clearly evident in this book's photographs, and I would like to thank him for his willingness to model and his continued friendship. Also for assistance with the photography I would like to thank Brad Jones sensei and Jon Juffs; Kevin Doherty sensei, James Hatch and the members of Ajax Budokan; Mitch Kawasaki sensei, Clint Partridge and the members of Kawasaki's Rendokan Judo Academy; Robert Zimmermann sensei and the members of Toronto Aikikai; John McCulloch sensei and the black belts of Shorinji Kempo Toronto Branch; and again, Kim A. Taylor sensei. I would also like to thank the administration of Toronto's Japanese Canadian Cultural Centre and several of its resident schools, including Osamu Obata shihan, Jim Wright and the members of the JCCC Aikikai; the members of Seidokai Judo; and the members of the JCCC Kendo Club.

A final offering of thanks and love is owed to my partner Sarah Stewart for her help, patience, humor and support during the three years it took to realize this volume.

Preface

I CAUGHT A LUCKY BREAK when I was eight years old. My father, who was then thirty-eight and beginning to sense he might lose the race to keep his high school track and field physique, signed up for karate classes at a local "chop-shop." The instructors were Caucasian, the school was non-profit, but the workout was good, and so was the reputation of the style's chief instructor— a Japanese man who inspired a mixture of respect, fantastical storytelling and not a little terror among his students, especially the eight-year-olds.

I say I was lucky because my father could have joined another school in our suburb, all too easily given the advertising of the commercially driven competitors at the time. I have often wondered how different my life might have been had my father (with my sister, my twin brother and myself in tow) signed up for a westernized, bottom-dollar-driven version of karate. A version of lesser pedigree, and quite possibly, of lesser substance. Would I have continued training into adulthood? Would I have been the same person, learned the same lessons?

The motivations for devoting a lifetime to studying an art, and the effects of those motivations on the practitioner partly inspired this book. Entering my third decade of training, and sensing the end of my own race with athletic achievement, I find myself increasingly curious about the differences between those who commit a lifetime to the martial arts, and those who begin the journey, but never see it through. What is it, I wondered, the latter group misses?

Not only is this book inspired by the *question* of what lies ahead for the committed practitioner, it is also inspired by those best able to *answer* the question—the unique people who have devoted their lives to the martial arts. Above all, this is a book about people. Having experienced first-hand the depth, sincerity, spontaneity and wisdom of my own teacher, I gambled (rightly in the case of the fifteen masters interviewed in this volume) that in those who devoted their lives to the ideals of the martial arts there would be universal traits—whether a natural result of age, or an inclination to devotion, or of long, serious inquiry of any kind, martial or not.

This book is also concerned with the inevitable loss of these people, for they are a unique generation.

Like the rest of Japanese society, Japanese martial arts were enormously impacted by the events of World War II. The militarism still present in many martial arts schools today traces most conspicuously to the building of Japan's war machine and the

nationalism that perverted many of the country's institutions—
a development deeply resented by the Japanese public following
the war's conclusion. The occupation of Japan by Allied forces
further impacted Japanese martial arts, first through the ban
instituted on all *budo*—martial ways—by General MacArthur's
General Headquarters of the Supreme Command for the Allied
Powers, but also through the exposure of western servicemen and
women to Japanese culture. (Karate was the one exception to the
ban, as it was misunderstood as simply a form of Chinese boxing.)
Although Japanese martial arts had spread around the world
through the immigration of the Japanese, the arts were largely
confined to expatriate communities, and unknown to the general
populace (judo being the possible sole exception). By the end
of Japan's occupation, on April 28, 1952, by decree of the San
Francisco Peace Treaty, a wave of non-Japanese ambassadors of
the martial arts—the Allied troops, many of whom had received
martial arts instruction—returned to the Western world.

Following close behind was the first contingent of Japanese
martial arts instructors, sent to establish official presence around
the globe, and to foster the spread of various newly formed or
re-formed martial arts associations and styles. Many of these
instructors had learned directly from the originators of their
art: from Gichin Funakoshi, the father of modern karate; from

Jigoro Kano, the founder of judo; and from Morihei Ueshiba, the founder of aikido. Having experienced the earliest incarnations of their arts, these first international instructors were aware of the original intents, motives and contexts under which the arts were developed.

The abuse of the martial arts during the war led to a recommitment to the ideals of *budo* as a means of self-cultivation. Indeed, the war itself—and the horrors of war—were instrumental in the development of Shorinji Kempo by its founder, Doshin So, who sought to restore the pride and self-respect of the Japanese people amidst the devastation of post-war Japan. While the non-violent ideals of *budo* are still professed in today's sport-oriented martial arts communities, I wonder if they will remain as prescient once the experience of the war passes from living memory? That experience also profoundly influenced Japanese–North Americans, four of whom are included in this volume.

Sadly, it is this generation of martial arts masters—who trained under the originators of their arts, who were transformed by the experience of World War II, who pioneered the globalization of modern Japanese martial arts—that is dying.

The masters included in this volume share two traits: They all practice a form of *gendai budo*—modern Japanese martial ways—and they have all continued that practice throughout their lifetime. Some are political figures, or hold the highest rank in their art; some represent historically significant family lineage; others built notable sporting careers, or pioneered the spread of the martial arts in a new corner of the world. All of them deserve to be celebrated.

Regrettably, no book could capture the contributions of all the World War II martial arts masters alive today. The masters who are included should not be considered spokespeople for their art (although a few do act officially in that capacity) or as premiere exponents of skill, accomplishment or position, as any such selection would be arbitrary at best. Rather, these fifteen masters represent (besides who was willing to be interviewed, was available to be interviewed and to whom I had an introduction) a cross-section of the experience possible during a lifetime study of modern Japanese martial arts.

The emphasis on personal experience over technical matters, and the fact that not all disciplines of *gendai budo* are represented in this volume, underscore its non-encyclopedic aim. Just as the journey from student to master involves unexpected meetings, unrepeatable events, unique experiences and surprising turns, so too are these interviews presented: unbound by formula.

My own equally serendipitous journey to interview these masters began with a search for active, war-era martial artists.

Guided by numerous researchers, academics and senior students of the disciplines, and with the all-important introductions of a few well-known Japanese instructors, I cultivated a series of connections and recommendations that led me, almost blindly, from one master to the next. Over a two-year period I traveled to Toronto, Ottawa, Seattle, Los Angeles, San Francisco, London, Paris and twice to Tokyo. Although Japan is—appropriately—represented most heavily in the book, I felt it was important to search out masters in North American and European countries, to reflect the worldwide spread of Japanese martial arts, and to include opinions on the training methods and experiences of Western students, whom I envisioned as the principle audience. Although I did employ a professional interpreter in Japan, who later reviewed my transcripts of the interviews using my audio recordings of each event, close students, and in some instances, family members of the masters who spoke English as a second language, helped clarify their ideas.

Accompanying the words of the masters is a collection of photographs that are figurative, rather than literal. My intent was to capture the aesthetics of the classical martial arts. An unfinished, unpolished quality to the imagery, a counterpoint to the masters' presence in the book, is meant to imply the learning process itself. Each unique moment of practice, the importance of the feeling within a motion, the need for students to be led organically to their own unique expression—all themes touched upon in the interviews—are, at their most ambitious, themes also reflected in the photographs. The images play a final role in the book by underscoring its implied thesis, when, hopefully, they speak to the common essence that lies beneath the martial arts' disparate surfaces.

Universal appeal among martial artists was certainly one of the early goals of this volume. But at its conclusion, it is clear that the thoughts of the fifteen remarkable men and women contained here far outreach the martial arts community. While this volume is the very antithesis of a martial arts textbook, it remains a manual nonetheless—a manual for a way of living, compiled from fifteen lifetimes spent living the Way.

Nobuyuki Kamogawa

KYUDO

Nobuyuki Kamogawa was born on September 25, 1923, in Nagasaki, Japan, and began his career in kyudo in 1936. He graduated from naval accounting school in 1945, and in 1965 established his own company, the Nishi-Nihon Data Service Company Limited. In 1973, he won the Technical Excellence Award in the all Japan kyudo tournament, competing in the *kyoshi* division, and has won the Nagasaki Sport Award five times.

Kamogawa has compiled the *Kyudo Manual* for the All Nippon Kyudo Federation (ANKF), as well as various other textbooks on kyudo. Since 1972, he has held annual seminars in Europe and is largely responsible for kyudo's subsequent rise in popularity there.

In 1976, he was conferred the *hanshi* title, and in 1992, he became the president of the All Japan Kyudo Federation. The following year, he opened the first kyudo seminar in the USA and was awarded kyudo's highest rank, tenth degree.

KOJIKI, THE OLDEST and the most important historical book in Japan, contains the accounts of "Japanese Mythology" in the volume *Age of the Gods.* The book describes the spectacular accounts of the birth of Japan and the whole of creation. According to it, Ameno-minakanushi-no-kami, the creator of the universe, created the boundless, extensive heaven and earth ages ago. Many ancient gods appeared after the creator of the universe, the god Izanagino-kami and the goddess Izanamino-kami among them. Amaterasu-omikami, the sun goddess, was born from Izanagino-kami and Izanamino-kami and became a creator of the country. The fifth generation of the sun goddess became a human being, Emperor Jinmu, the first emperor of Japan.

The country was not united at that time and savage tribes thrived. Emperor Jinmu took to the field to conquer them, but was confronted with very tough battles. One day, while he was fighting, a golden kite—a bird—flew down from heaven, resting at the tip of the arrow in his hand. Then the tip of the arrow started to glitter. In a moment, the savage soldiers were dazzled and defeated. This account, written in *Kojiki,* led to the adoption

of the arrow in the emperor's emblem, and later the arrow was used as a ritualistic implement.

Needless to say, people used the arrow for hunting in ancient times, and it was also used as a weapon during the warring periods. But after the introduction of firearms by the Portuguese in 1543, the bow and arrow lost their advantage as a weapon. However, with the influence of the teachings of Confucius, which was introduced to Japan from China, the bow and arrow were used as instruments to foster the soul and spirit of samurai, to discipline the samurai mentally and physically. Thus, the arrow has been a spiritual stay for the Japanese since the

age of the Warring States Period (1477–1573). *Kyujutsu*, the art of archery, became kyudo, the way of archery, and is now used to build character, to discipline body and mind. Of course, that can be said for all other Japanese martial arts as well. After the Second World War, Japan was in a state of confusion and the family system disintegrated—its base was destroyed. Moral education was not given to students at school, so the martial arts made a great contribution in restoring a sense of morality.

People say that we should have freedom and equality, but freedom and equality have to be accompanied by responsibility.

It is a basic idea, yet not widely held. I think the martial arts can contribute to an understanding of this sort of concept. All martial arts are considered to start and end with courtesy, and it is from this position that we should claim our freedom and equality. Modern archery is said to be a kind of sport. Yes, it is certainly a competitive sport—by hitting the target, people can win or lose. But it is also a way of disciplining the mind and body. Winners shouldn't boast, and the people who lost shouldn't be humiliated, if possible. As long as archery is sought as a way, you have to be considerate toward others. Progress should be made together, with warmness of heart, with consideration.

I was born in 1923 and started archery around 1935. When I was a child, the population practicing kyudo was very small because kyudo was very, very strict. Even the most basic education took many long hours; I spent an entire year acquiring only basic skills. For six months, I was restricted to practicing my form and cleaning up the dojo and the *azuchi*, where the targets were kept. I used to pull arrows from the targets for the senior students too. After that, I was finally allowed to begin real shooting, but only on straw practice targets. I did that for one year—a whole year. Back then, if five people began practicing with the straw targets, by the end of the year, only one person remained.

If I went about my teaching the same way today, nobody would be left. To attract people, we have to keep their interest—they're not patient, they can't wait, they get bored and give up—so we have to adjust our methods. My teachers used to say to us that whenever we got bored, we should leave immediately. That's how I was taught when I was a child, but this trend has changed greatly over time. People who have trained as I did, very hard and very strictly, people who have trained before the world war, don't lose their base. Their foundation in archery is very firm, their form is very solid. Even if they stop shooting for ten years or more, they can keep their form. I can see whether they had been trained hard before, whether they had studied as I had, by looking at them.

When teaching a student, I look at their bone structure and character, and I create a tailored plan for them. However, some

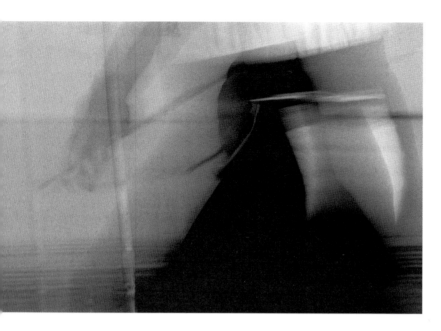

young people already have a little experience shooting and want to stick to the ways they are used to. It's very hard for them to start a new way of training—they cannot give up what they have learned and studied. Although it *is* important for them to keep what they already know, they cannot accept a new way of teaching with an open mind. I see this phenomenon among many young students. I tell them that they should try the new method for at least two weeks. Gradually, if they continue, they will find interest in it, and then, after two or three months, they will have forgotten the sort of shooting they had practiced in the past. I always emphasize this point when I teach.

As I mentioned before, the teacher shouldn't proceed in one set way. He should know the student well, should consider their individual structure and character, and draw them to the direction that's best for them, not to the direction the teacher likes. For example, imagine a road with a destination. A student is walking, but in the wrong direction, and the teacher, watching him, suggests that he take a turn in the proper direction. But it's already too late. I think the teacher should have suggested changing direction prior to that point, before the student was far off track.

So a good teacher will walk his student back. The student will think he is being taught basic things, things he has already studied that he considers at too low a level for him. Even still, the good teacher knows he should return to that stage so the student can then make a straight passage. Otherwise, the teacher makes two mistakes by not correcting what he should have noticed in the beginning. So with courage, you have to teach to return to the right place. The teacher should be courageous and confident enough to take the student back to the right place, to go back. In actuality, it's not a going back but another process of progress. That is how I see it.

When the Tokyo Olympics were held in 1964, I was a representative of Japan. I gave a demonstration, an exhibition, and many people praised my beautiful form. At that time, I was thirty-eight or thirty-nine years old—almost half of my present age—and I was very boastful when everyone gathered around me. However, as I got older, my shooting strength got weaker and I suffered from cancer and went through three operations. My sickness affected my skill and my concept of archery a lot. When I was full of pride, I didn't see the bad points in my technique or in myself. But gradually the mistakes piled up, the amount of time I had for practice was reduced, and slowly my form declined. When I noticed this, I had to think over what I had done. I thought of the future, and gradually my way of thinking changed. I realized that as long as I was boastful, I was not reaching the height of the lessons in kyudo. Archery educates—teaches you how to live. Kyudo teaches a very serious way of life.

I was born in Nagasaki prefecture. The Nagasaki dialect has a word, *kanmaji*, that my teacher used to say. The way he used the word, it meant "to draw your arrow, minding nothing." That means that when you shoot, you don't mind whether you hit the target or not. You cannot think with reason, you have to empty your mind and commit to yourself. Draw your arrow with an empty state of mind. Using a bow is seeking what the heart of the bow seeks. You have to seek the Way in it. *Kanmaji*. Don't mind anything else, just concern yourself with shooting. I always remember my teacher saying this.

The bow must be drawn with abdominal strength. Breathe deeply, from your soul. Breathing is very important. In the case of archery, we call it *iki-ai*, "how to breathe." It must be very relaxed, so that the mind, body and arrow unite into one. That's the state of mind I want to attain, that I want my students to attain as well. You cannot be affected by emotion.

In kyudo, we say that you should be of service to others without seeking compensation or reward for yourself. Kyudo, for me, is a kind of religion. I try not to seek rewards. *Inga oho*. What

Using a bow is seeking what the heart of the bow seeks.

goes around comes around—this is how I cultivate myself. We don't expect students to understand the technical aspects only, because winning or losing is not a priority. When you win, then you become boastful, as my experience has taught me. You can easily recognize whether the archer hit the target or not. But this is not what we should be judging for success. There are challenges prior to this stage. Did the archer tackle kyudo with an empty mind, one that will create a healthy body and healthy mind? That is the Way that kyudo is seeking—whether the archer has contributed to a healthy society. Of course there are targets to shoot, to aim for, but hitting the target is not the final goal. In kyudo we say, "Shoot at your heart"—shoot at your conscious thoughts. Whether it is recognized properly by other people or not, you yourself must recognize whether you exerted the utmost effort toward the target. How many arrows were shot is not important—the contents of those arrows is what counts.

Hidetaka Nishiyama

KARATE-DO

Hidetaka Nishiyama was born on October 10, 1928, in Tokyo and began training with the founder of modern karate, Gichin Funakoshi, in 1943. In 1951, Nishiyama co-founded the Japan Karate Association (JKA). His book *Karate: The Art of Empty-Hand Fighting* was published in 1960. The following year, on a trip to the United States, he created the All American Karate Federation (AAKF).

Nishiyama organized the first international karate competition in 1965, and co-founded and was elected chairman of the Pan-American Karate Union (PAKU) in 1973. Two years later, the International Amateur Karate Federation (IAKF) held its first world championship in Los Angeles. Now known as the International Traditional Karate Federation (ITKF), the organization is still under Nishiyama's direction and has over seventy member countries worldwide.

In November 2000, the Emperor of Japan awarded Nishiyama the Fourth Order of Merit, and he was decorated with the Order of the Sacred Treasure for his contributions to the promotion of Japanese culture. Nishiyama sensei currently holds the rank of ninth-degree black belt.

I AM STILL A STUDENT, not a master. I started martial arts training when I was five years, five months and five days old. That is the custom in a samurai family. My father woke me up, put a kendo uniform on me and took me to the dojo. Then, when I was sixteen, I switched to karate, and I've continued with it until today. I found it more interesting, more difficult, harder to understand. I like kendo very much, but for some reason I don't like any sport that has something in between my body and what I'm doing. I like the body movement. Karate has no other weapon except the body—it's very interesting.

I think a young start is good. The most important thing for coaching children is motivation, how to motivate their training. For instance, a kid might come up to me and say they like Superman. So I'll say, "Oh, yeah? You like Superman? Let's pretend we're him." Then the child will be interested. But if you just teach the techniques, they'll be yawning. So the instructor's job must be to keep motivation high. Find games that will help with technique. Make sure they enjoy it, then teach them the proper way. During *seiza*, they can study concentration.

In Japan, they have a word to describe good martial arts teachers: *shinan*. *Shi* is finger, *nan* is south. Together they mean "pointing south," like a compass. A bad instructor says, "Like me, this way," teaching students to copy them. *Shinan* isn't like that. *Shinan* means you must show the proper direction to the student so they can develop themselves. I like this word, *shinan*. It came originally from the Chinese.

I was very lucky when I started my training. It was wartime and many of my seniors went off to fight but never came back. And many of the older seniors reacted badly to the war. Their hearts were not in their training and they weren't serious. For a short time, I was in the navy, but I came back and continued to practice. So there was really only these older ranks and me, and very quickly I had to take on many responsibilities, coaching at schools and colleges and so on. It was a good chance for me to meet many masters. I met Mr. Shioda. He was Mr. Ueshiba's [founder of aikido] top student, so he would often bring me to Ueshiba sensei's dojo and we would talk about martial arts. I was very lucky to meet so many top martial artists. Many times I was shown *kata* and was able to discuss things with them. Used to be that someone like me would have no chance even to meet top people like that. But because wartime circumstances placed me among the top ranks, I was able to have this communication.

The first day I started training at Funakoshi sensei's dojo, we faced the wall with our legs open, down low in *kibadachi*, for two hours. There was no instruction—he was trying to make us understand with our bodies, not with logic. Training systems today have developed many good ideas, and we use them to improve reaction time and develop certain areas. These days, people can quite easily be coached for quick development and to look good on the outside. But the down side is that inside they are very weak. The study of combat

techniques is supposed to make a strong, fighting person. The techniques don't have to be fancy. Of course, skill is important—I coach many technical points—but people get caught up wanting to learn more and more techniques. The result is that no one technique is ever made strong enough. In the time of swords, people usually used only one, there was no need for ten swords. The question is how to use one sword, how to use one punch.

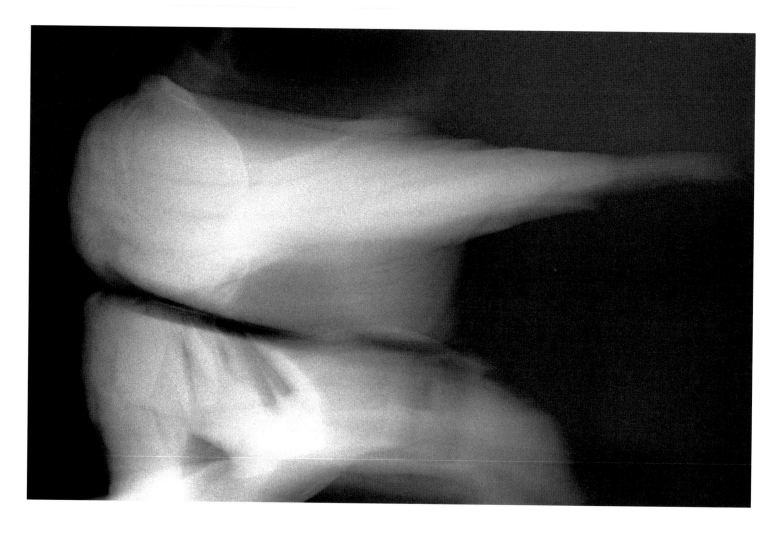

This is important. But it seems no matter how strongly I tell people this, they want more and more techniques for their outside appearance. They learn one *kata*, then they ask me to teach another, then another. Okay, they've learned thirty—they know it all. No, this is just external.

It used to be that karate was stronger but, of course, not so fancy. So today we have good technical instruction, but the results are not strong enough. In *budo*, you need to make one technique strong. It was the same when I studied sword. I liked one technique, *kote-zuki*. Every day I would practice it. Of course, during matches, I would vary my techniques, but mainly I used that one, because of the self-confidence it gave me. If I had a hundred techniques, I wouldn't be sure which to use. In karate, we are lucky to have so many techniques, but at the same time we are unlucky because we have too many. So I coach my students to find a favorite technique they can practice over and over again, in their sleep, until they understand it. Then they can move on to a second technique, then another, one by one. I tell them not to become weapon collectors. Weapon collectors have one sword, then ten swords, then a hundred swords, but don't know how to use any of them.

Karate originally came from China, and their ideas are a little different from Japan's. The Chinese like variety. When you go to a Chinese restaurant, it's very colorful. Japan is more simple. Like Japanese Shinto temples—they have ordinary wood, no color. The Chinese are more fancy; the Japanese are more simple. So Japanese martial arts try to cut out all unnecessary movements.

From the external actions of *kata*, you learn the principles behind them. When you learn the principles, you can understand their correct application. But when the motions are changed over

the course of a single generation, you can no longer reach those principles that have been developed over hundreds of years and many generations of masters. *Kata* uses outside techniques to seek inner principles. If we change those techniques, it's like a compass that has lost its direction.

I have studied the *kata* exactly as master Funakoshi taught them. Of course, in my training, I have digested many points myself and so it looks a little different—everyone has a different body—but the principles are the same. Coaching the exact ideas of master Funakoshi is my job. Seeking is the student's job. But if the outside is changed, the direction will be lost. Maybe today I understand this much. Maybe tomorrow I understand a little more—if I practice. But I won't have the chance to understand the principles if I change the outside techniques. Yet this is what is happening, and this is why tradition is important.

In Japan, there are three stages of learning, called *shu ha ri*— protect, diverge, separate. You follow the movements of your teacher, then slowly you begin to understand more for yourself—

not mentally, but through the physical digestion of the techniques. At the *sandan* level, I don't coach outside movements. I look to the body and only coach principles. Of course, I touch up some basic points, but fundamentally the different *kata* and different styles all share the same principles: posture, muscle control, mental power, breathing, how breathing controls the muscles— these kinds of things.

Mentally, it's very important to keep stable emotions. This comes from the self-confidence gained through training. It's essential to be able to make the proper judgment and have the proper reaction to a situation. But this part of training is not so serious now. It used to be there were real fights, real confrontations where you faced life and death. If your training wasn't good, you would die. Well, people need to train with that sort of seriousness today. Here's a common example: If you had a school examination tomorrow, you would naturally study very hard. It's the same thing, the same mindset. Then, with that kind of seriousness, you begin to approach the level of art.

Finally—this is an old martial arts idea—the one who wins the fight is of the lowest class. The one that wins without fighting is best. The one that fights maybe wins, maybe loses. But without fighting, you never lose. You train and work hard and finally there is self-development. Then, when you face your opponent, they

I always keep the idea, not only in karate but in the rest of my life, that tomorrow will be better than yesterday.

become scared of your strength and you stop their actions. This is best.

Today there is very strong development of karate in the former Soviet Union. They have a strong spirit. Once they start karate, they don't give up—just karate, that's their attitude. They never change.

In the West, people run back and forth and can't make up their minds. Too spoiled. In Japan too, that's my feeling, too spoiled. Lots of money, money, money. They don't like hard training. They want to know the easiest, shortest way to black belt. I can go to a sporting-goods store and buy a black belt for two or three dollars. But people in the Soviet Union never think this way. So when the economy is good, human life is better, but we also get spoiled. This is not so good for martial arts.

I grew up during wartime. When I started to train, I trained for my country, for Japan, for the Emperor, for something to die for. But after the war ended, everything completely changed. What had given me a sense of justice now left me feeling completely empty inside. My whole life, I had trusted something, and now it

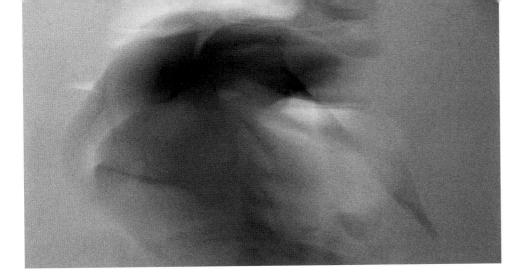

was gone. That's the reason I trained harder in karate—I was seeking a new justice. What else could I do?

I find it's the same thing in former communist countries today. People believed in communism, studied Lenin and Mao. Then suddenly they're told communism is bad, Lenin is bad, Stalin is a criminal. Of course, young people are empty. So when they start martial arts, I try to help these people use karate to fill up their emptiness through training.

I train every day, and I always keep the idea, not only in karate but in the rest of my life, that tomorrow will be better than yesterday. No matter what you face, whatever weakness or handicap, training gives you the courage to believe—better than yesterday, better than yesterday. This is how I feel. There will always be mistakes and successes. But mistakes are not bad, they are based on something, on an effort. This is trial and error. If you are afraid, you'll never try. But you must try.

Hanae Sawada

ATARASHII NAGINATA

Hanae Sawada was born on July 21, 1916, and began her lifelong study of naginata at the age of eight. After graduating from Tennoji Women's High School in 1934, she enrolled in a training school for naginata teachers at the All Japan Martial Arts Federation, then began teaching naginata at women's high schools.

She was the first president of the Tokyo Naginata Association, a position she held from 1958 to 1966, and she has been a panel judge for the All Japan Naginata Federation since its inception in 1955.

In 1977, Sawada was granted the title of *hanshi*. She has been awarded the Governor of Tokyo Award and a number of distinguished service medals for her contribution to sport. Hanae Sawada is currently the president of the Shinjuku Naginata Association. She lives in Tokyo.

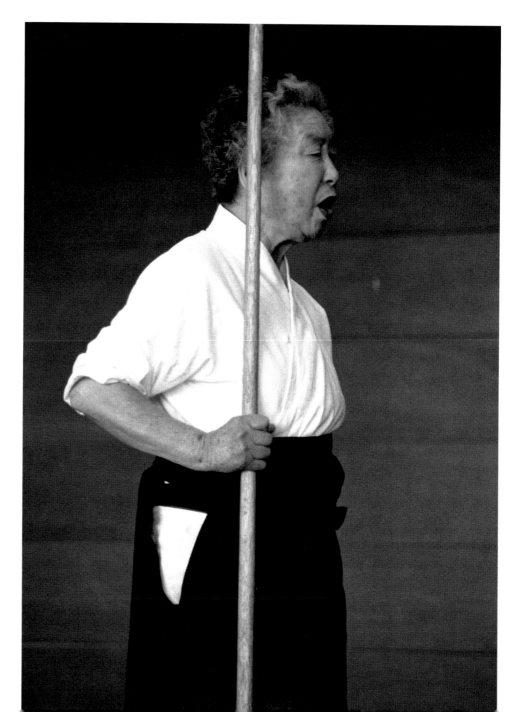

THERE WAS A DOJO in my family's home when I was a child. My father was a kendo instructor. I watched the classes when I was very young and soon started practicing. When I was taught, kendo, judo, iaido, naginata, karate—they were all mixed together, all taught as one. It was the same in the feudal age. The old warrior samurais practiced all the martial arts. They could do them all.

My instructor's name was Chiyo Mitamura. She never spoke during class—made no comments at all. If you were a beginner, she would explain a little, but while practice was carried out, she was practicing too. She didn't say you should correct this or correct that. Nothing. She would just look at us—and we could tell from that whether she was pleased or not. She was very strict. There were twenty-one students in the class, all levels, so we would strain to listen to her when she spoke to the more senior ranks, and at the same time, we would watch those who were the best in the class. It was a very good lesson for me, not to get any comments from the teacher. She taught me to learn from my own experience, to find out about naginata for myself. And I did, little by little. Other people finished the basic course in one year, but because my father was a kendo teacher, he made me continue with the basics for four years.

When I was young, I became very ill and developed pleurisy. I nearly died. When I closed my eyes, I thought all the air was coming out of my lungs—I was terribly scared. I felt lost and didn't know what to do. So I recalled my naginata form. We have a pushing motion, and I thought of that, holding the naginata very firmly and pushing back. There were no other thoughts in my mind, just this action. I tried to make my state of mind the same as the motion itself. I was very scared, the air still felt like it was coming out, but I tried to forget, I tried to think of nothing except grabbing the naginata very firmly. I was half dead—halfway to the other world. I dreamed somebody was behind me, telling me about the beautiful flowers there, telling me I should go. I could hear them calling from behind me, telling me how beautifully clean the water was.

It took me half a year to recover. I was bedridden. I couldn't walk because my circulation was so poor. I realized that I was going to survive when I felt the coldness of a garden stepping stone. I felt it, and that gave me the first sense that I might recover. All the time that I was alone and in bed, I tried to concentrate my attention on naginata, nothing else. That was

what I learned then: the importance of mental concentration. So without naginata, I feel that I couldn't have survived. And after that, I decided I had to practice very hard.

Without naginata, it's possible I would have turned out to be a bad person. My conscience, my will, was concentrated on practicing naginata itself, so I didn't have room to consider other things. When I look around at other people, I think that the same could be said of other martial arts too, not only naginata. You can see it. When I am watching a kendo practice, I can tell what stage they are at. And when watching judo, I can guess, I can see what stage they are at, both technically and mentally, by the way they move.

I think students are the best judge of what makes a good teacher. It depends on the individual, whether they prefer to have a teacher who can give a lot of advice or one who doesn't talk too much. It's perhaps better to stay with one teacher, because a long period of time is required to establish a relationship and otherwise the teacher cannot know the personality and the character of the student. My students also practice at other dojos, and so they hear many different ideas. One teacher says this is good, another one doesn't—all teachers have different opinions. So because I know my students well and know what stage they are at, I can give the proper advice to them, even though they have learned at other dojos. I was loyal to my one teacher, because I wanted to be like her. I would try to catch up with her and was inspired to study very hard. If you have many teachers, then it may be difficult to go one way, to know which way you should follow. If you want to be a better practitioner and you choose this teacher, and then you try another teacher to get better skills, it will be very difficult to improve. I myself practiced very hard to try to catch up to my teacher, but I think she is still far ahead of me. I still need more experience.

Competition means that you are competing with your opponent's mind or heart. You have to be trying, from the very first glance when you look at the person in the match, to see what she is thinking. You have to read your partner's mind when you step in to attack. That's the difference between third and fourth dan—your state of mind. It's the mind itself that's different, nothing technical. You must keep your mind clean. If you are in a match and begin thinking about what technique he or she might use, that means you are thinking extra things. It is very important to read your opponent's technique instead of going after it. If your mind is doing anything else, it's not practice. In addition, you have to have an agile response. If you react after being attacked, it will be too late. We practice using *bogu*, but on a real battlefield, you are always confronted with immediate death. So you have to be well prepared, get ready for any attack at any moment.

While you are learning basic forms, you don't think anything. But gradually, as you advance, you begin to consider various strategies, so you begin to think. But at the final stage, eventually you have to put yourself back to keeping nothing in your mind. The most important thing is to return to the basics. At first you are wrapped up in just learning basics, nothing occupies your mind except learning. After a while, you'll begin to think various things, but ultimately you must come back to that first step. Think nothing.

I used to practice *zazen*, Zen meditation. One day, while I was meditating, I experienced all the serenity I could attain. I felt as if I had been meditating on top of a mountain. I wasn't concerned with anything. It was a purified state, with nothing intruding into my mind. I was united with nature, had experienced it in oneness. You need teachers in learning anything. You may have many confrontations with other people, but through those experiences, you can grow your dream. You'll learn a lot of things by communicating with other people. They are your teachers as well in many ways.

Human beings have two ways of breathing: breathing out and breathing in. Whenever there is another person, there is communication, there is a current, inhalation and exhalation.

You have to be flexible enough to follow when you learn. Practice what you have learned repeatedly, and then your mind will become pure. So practice whatever your teacher taught you many times until you acquire it yourself. Through repetition and practice, your mind will be changed too. I can see the changes at the different stages. If a person at fourth dan is promoted to fifth dan, I can see the difference in them, although it is the same person. By repeating exactly, going back and forth and back and forth, gradually, eventually, they can attain the very advanced stage.

Now, one person may practice up to this stage and consider that's enough for him. Another person may go back and forth and back and forth, and little by little attains the very highest level. Look at a big tree. It didn't have a big trunk from the beginning. It started from a sapling, and then, over a period of years, the trunk grew, and the tree developed extensive branches and roots. The tree cannot grow to that state all at one time—it needs years and years. The same thing can be said of human beings. You cannot be promoted or advanced to the highest rank at one time. You need practice. To put yourself instantly into the correct form, with no hesitation, you need a lot of practice.

I have nothing to regret. So many men, so many minds, but this I know: By pursuing one objective, you'll be able to find your real destination. I myself am still trying to make my mind as pure as I can and to contribute to make society peaceful. I think the martial arts, in Japan's case, have been handed down through the generations from heart to heart. They are communicated through the heart. That's why they have survived.

I appreciate very much the time I have had with my students when I didn't think anything at all and just practiced with them. Sometimes I practiced with one woman, another time someone else—each one was different, and my mind was different depending on the student. I cannot teach in the same state of mind with different people. Everyone is at a different level, so I have to pull their heart toward me, each in a different way. And I'm very lucky to enjoy those moments. They are the happiest thing I can recall. Today, during practice, each woman shouted a command, and each shouted differently, but they were united while they practiced, and I pulled them all toward me. When I taught, at one time, more than fifty people, I could pull all of their different minds toward me, united into one. That was the happiest moment I ever had. It's not a matter of simply yelling or shouting at the students, I am trying to pull them, their state of mind, toward me. A teacher has to lead, has to be able to draw students in. There are many happy things that we can enjoy in the world. By practicing something in a group, the joy itself is different depending on the individuals.

...the joy itself is different depending on the individuals.

I am now leaving naginata to my students. I can't ask them to follow or observe my ideas. Each one of them learned the same lessons from me but has interpreted them under different circumstances. I give many comments and advice to my students, even though my teacher didn't give me any advice at all. Some time ago, I broke my leg. Before that, I didn't say much, I waited for them to learn. But I can't wait any longer. Compared with me, my students started very late. I am old and I want them to reach the master stage as soon as possible. I don't have much time. I used to tell them that they have to find out about naginata for themselves, but I'm getting old and there is much for them to learn. I cannot wait for them. So I've started yelling.

Masao Takahashi

JUDO

Masao Takahashi was born in 1929 in Stave Falls, British Columbia. He began his training in judo in Vancouver at a Japanese-language school at the age of eight. He enlisted in the Royal Canadian Air Force in 1949 and was subsequently stationed in eastern Canada, Germany and Japan, where he trained NATO soldiers in judo. In 1969, he opened the Takahashi Dojo in Ottawa. His four children are all black belts in judo. Two of them are three-time Olympians (one in wrestling), and one was an Olympic coach.

In 1984, Takahashi was named a Life Member by Judo Canada and has been inducted into the Canadian Forces Sports Honour Roll, the Judo Canada Hall of Fame and the Judo Ontario Hall of Fame, and was recently conferred the Order of the Sacred Treasure, Gold Rays with Rosette, from the Emperor of Japan. Takahashi sensei has also trained a little in karate, aikido and kendo, and currently holds the rank of eighth-degree black belt in judo.

THE OLD SAYING IS, if your enemy is attacking, let him fight uphill with the sun looking into his eyes. You have to use those kinds of principles. The way judo was explained to me was that in olden times, fights occurred in the mountains, and fighters, tiring from being lopsided, gravitated down into the swamp. So judo is swamp or bog fighting. All your holds are designed so the victim—the loser—is belly up and the winner can escape anytime. These are the ways the technical rules were made. I can get away from you, but the one that's caught in the hold can't—he's drowning.

Most novices who fight in tournaments have already lost, because of anxiety. Let's say they're fighting on the weekend. They worry about it all week when what they should do is check out the place. You have to know your mountain, you have to know every rock, every water hole, where the clearing is in the forest. In the olden days, you didn't know what kind of place you were going to fight in. Today you've got these fancy mats—they're all the same now. But back then they didn't know what they had. It might be the plastic mats that slip—you could use that for an excuse, "Geez, you know, I slipped." And it's true, you did slip.

But you should still go check out the place, look at the lighting. Because some of these guys are a wreck, they spook in front of a crowd, but other guys are in really good shape.

You go and check your mountain, the clearing where you're going to fight. This is very important. If you become the champion, you get the medal and everybody claps, but you are not to feel that you are the most superior— you are the least incompetent. You were just lucky enough to be the least incompetent that time.

Sports broadcasters don't know what to ask an athlete. The first question is always, "How are your injuries?" That's the focus. Every Canadian likes to talk about injuries. But the Japanese are different. You watch professional sumo wrestlers, they're like poker players: They don't crack a smile, they're not supposed to. Every time anybody asks them a question, they say, "I'm doing the best I can. I'm striving to do the best I can."

The Hollywood image might have glamorized judo, but I think it confuses a lot of people, a lot of young kids. Sport has changed the fighting rules for the worse too. When I used to fight, they never had these weight classes, so it was *fun*. Now, every year—bang!—there's seven national men's champions and seven national women's champions. Judo wasn't designed for that. We know that before long there will be ten weight classes, like in amateur wrestling.

Now that we've gone that route, we have to make the best of it. We have to go along. The Europeans organized their votes and changed the rules—in my opinion, too much and too soon. Of course, if you make it a sport, that's what happens. I'm not sad about it—it's evolution, like anything else. We all belong to one great organization. Judo is accepted by the International Olympic Committee and has been in the games since 1964, and that gave it a big rise in popularity. We have more countries in the International Judo Federation than in the United Nations. So I guess it's okay as a sport. I mean, it's harmless.

We call judo a sport, but, really, it's the study of a culture. Of course, if we ask people if they'd like to learn some culture,

> We call judo a sport, but, really, it's the study of a culture.

no one's likely to be too interested. But if we call it a sport, people are more willing to take a look at it. Besides, everything has to evolve. Maybe judo has become overly sport-oriented, but it's like glaciers in the olden days. It wasn't just one sheet of ice that covered the northern hemisphere; several advanced and retreated, back and forth. Well, I think things will change again soon.

I would have preferred judo to have gone the other way from sport, you might say a more fundamental way, the way Kano shihan would have wanted it to be. The thing is, there's money to be made, and if there's money to be made, people will manufacture all kinds of different styles of martial arts—which is happening. There are a lot of dojos that come and go, mainly because they can't pay the rent, which is fair. What's happening here today already happened in Japan a hundred and thirty or forty years ago. They went through the kinds of throes that we're going through now: dojos that can't pay the rent, mixtures of styles, associations that are no good. It'll all come out in the wash. I think the future looks good for all of the martial arts.

My daughter Tina won the gold medal at the World University Championships in 1983, and became the first Canadian to win a world judo title. I'm very proud of her. My children will run the dojo eventually. But, you know, the way I look at it and the way my kids look at it is different. They're the ones who fell through the cracks. I didn't really start my dojo to develop champions or Olympians, I just wanted them to participate because I thought it was a good thing. But when carding came along, that kind of changed me. Carding means they were given money by the government. They got training fees and a living allowance for bringing home medals from international competitions. And they got to go to university too—all my kids went through that. I was a low paid airman, then a flight engineer, and I wasn't making a whole pile of money in the military. Now they are teachers, and I think they're anxious to produce champions themselves. I don't know if I can get that out of them.

Following every last bit of etiquette in the dojo is a little too "Japanese"—especially for white teachers who believe in discipline but tend to overdo it at times. Some instructors might interpret it as a power trip—and that would be a disaster. If a person has the right attitude and they're not there to perform parlor tricks, they can really enjoy the martial arts and become good citizens. Every country has some sort of martial art, and those that participate in it don't have to become champions. As my mother said, "You don't have to win the cup. In fact, I prefer that you lose."

Pierre Trudeau, the former Canadian prime minister, said the same thing. He trained here, his three sons too. I learned a lot about myself knowing that gentleman. He was modest and humble. When his son competed in his first tournament, he told me he was glad to see him lose. Most fathers like to see their children win because their kid is an extension of themselves. But not Mr. Trudeau. Like my mother, he knew there were lessons to be learned. He'd rough it up with the kids and do all kinds of falls for them—he really knew how to handle them. See, even if a kid knows how to fall, they don't like to; they'd rather be the one doing the throwing!

Judo is beautiful this way. You can go to the dojo with your best friend, but then for half an hour he becomes your most formidable enemy. That's called *randori*—free-style practice. Like Japanese police stations—they don't waste time fooling around. Whenever a police station is built, the first thing they do is create a big dojo so the people coming off shift or going on can hammer it out. Lots of private dojos in Japan are closing because these police halls have great facilities, and people send their children there to learn discipline. And the police are hard on them too.

Many are softies now—they try to get out of going. We sure
couldn't have tried that. But then I'm from a different generation.
I'm an oldie.

I would say half of the parents who come to my dojo think
judo is primarily for self-defense. They don't want their kids
beaten up in school or swarmed in an alley. They want them to
be capable of protecting themselves. In my time, the parents had

what's called a *koenkai*, basically a support group for the judo school. When they ran a tournament, all the parents and the families would come and donate money. They would write their names on a piece of paper and clip it to a clothesline. Whoever gave the most money had their name first. These days, a single mom will chauffeur the kid to the school, and if the child doesn't like it, mom says, "Well, that's okay, quit." We weren't conditioned that way. I don't know if anybody ever quit when we were young. You just didn't think of it. But in our day, there was nothing better to do. We didn't have TV. I would come home from school and then go to Japanese-language school and then go to judo.

When I read the papers and see what kids do today— smashing up headstones in cemeteries, all kinds of vandalism—I

think we were extra good as kids. I don't know if Japanese people could ever do those kinds of things. It's the Shinto in them that prevents that kind of behavior. Just as you can take the boy out of the farm but you can't take the farm out of the boy, it takes a long time to take the Shinto out of a Japanese kid.

Another thing a lot of people, especially young people, tend to do is compare the martial arts. They always want to know which is better, judo or karate or something else. I have a friend who is a priest. He takes care of a cemetery near my aunt. He would invite me in for saké and tell me all kinds of stories. He said if you have to compare the martial arts, compare them as a mountain to a river. The mountain, he said, should not look down on the river because it's lowly, and the river should not make fun of the mountain because it can't dance and move.

Pat Yoshitsugu Murosako

KENDO, IAIDO

Pat Murosako was born on January 2, 1921, in Fresno, California. He began kendo in 1935 and soon joined the Fresno Kendo Federation under Nakamura Tokichi. During World War II, he served with the Asiatic force, U.S. intelligence unit 520, in Japan.

After the war, he resumed his training and formed the Pasadena Buddhist Church Kendo Bu with Hara Akio. Murosako then became the first English secretary of the All United States Kendo Federation while the renowned kendoka Torao Mori—who became Murosako's first iaido instructor—was president. Murosako also helped form the Southern California Iaido Association and served as president of the Southern California Kendo Federation.

In 1985, Murosako sensei opened kendo and iaido schools after moving to Seattle, Washington. Currently, he holds a seventh dan in kendo and a sixth dan in iaido and is also an advisor for the Muso Shinden-Ryu Kenkyukai.

I WAS THROWN INTO JAIL so many times because of my color: Arizona, New Mexico, Kansas, Wisconsin. I was put in solitary confinement, for my own protection, I suppose, instead of in the drunk tank with the others, where I might have been beaten up. The sheriff used to come to where I worked and pick me up for questioning. I couldn't get a haircut at any barbershop, couldn't go to a restaurant. My only escape was to go to a movie at night, sit at the back and hope that nobody would see me. For an hour and a half, I could sit there and escape. There were some people who went out of their way to help me, but many more were too scared. It was like I had leprosy. I was probably the loneliest person in the whole damn world. It was a nightmare—being alone with nobody to talk to. I mostly lived in a dream, to get away. There were a few young boys that invited me to their place, but only so long as no other friends came. They were afraid. Even after I came out of the army, there was still prejudice—others just didn't want to associate with me.

What did I have to do to prove I was an American? Look at all the people like me, my age, that died in Europe and in the Philippines and in Borneo.

Most of the people like me who went to school worked "in the closet," as we used to say. We weren't allowed to work in the front. Our ability might have been good, but we never got a promotion. A white person would get all the credit for the work we did.

People didn't even want to sell us a home. We'd be invited to look at a house over the phone, but when we got there they wouldn't let us go inside. We knew right away. We could sense it. They would talk very nicely to us, then send us on our way.

It's surprising how narrow-minded people can be, how few people in the United States know anything about different nationalities, about anything other than the white race. I think the whole experience is probably part of what drives me. I've got culture. What do you have? I have a culture thousands of years old. I have a sword made in the early 1500s that I still use. What do you have? I'm an American in one way, but spiritually I'm really Japanese. I think many Japanese people are no more Japanese than their name and face. The same is true for many other nationalities also. They don't have any of their culture.

Kendo is the epitome of Japanese culture, so I wanted to continue with it. Being Japanese and not knowing anything about your culture is a shame. That goes for Mexican or French or any other country too. Today 99.9 percent of the people studying kendo are not Japanese, especially in America. In our iaido

group, we have about twenty students. Out of that twenty, there are about four Japanese students, and out of those four, only a couple speak Japanese. They're fourth generation, looking for their culture.

My life without kendo would have been aimless, ordinary. In my day, it didn't matter what you were attracted to, you went where your father told you. There was discipline. One day, he'd bring you to the dojo and say, "This is my son—take him." There were no ifs, ands or buts, no questions about whether you liked it or not—it was final. And I can tell you, I hated kendo. Oh, yeah. I wasn't crazy about kendo—wearing those dressy pants, looking like a girl. I used to walk through the alleys so nobody could see me. If my father knew that now, he'd roll over in his grave. But my sensei would be very proud, because I've lasted this long.

I trained with Nakamura Tokichi sensei. He would make you do kendo until you dropped. Teachers in Japan will push you a little more, a little more, up to a higher plateau. Kendo is like running a marathon. You don't run a whole one the first day. You run against your own time, testing your own mental stamina. Kendo is the same way. You practice and practice, maybe you last five minutes until you're totally exhausted and just can't do it anymore. Then, as time goes on, you're able to last six minutes, seven minutes. Finally, your instructor will start getting tired before you because you just don't stop. In other words, you've learned to cut off your exhaustion, your body exhaustion and your mind, completely. People can do that. First the mind says, "I'm tired, I'm tired," and of course you begin to believe you are tired. Then the next stage of exhaustion emerges—your body actually does begin to tire. That's the second stage. Then the third stage comes, the dangerous one. This is where the teacher has to know when to stop. Your organs, your heart, your gut, your insides begin to be exhausted and you throw up. The body refuses to go. No instructor should ever push a student to that stage, but occasionally you don't realize it and a student will pass out on you. So you have to watch out.

Etiquette is probably the most important part of kendo. You respect the sensei, no matter how strong you become. If you get stronger than your teacher, some people will tell you to go to another dojo and forget about the old sensei that started you off. No! Your sensei is always your sensei—no matter if your rank is higher. But that is slowly being lost, even in Japan. Now, sometimes a sensei will send you to another dojo because he can no longer teach you—he wants to send you to a better dojo. But that sensei is still your sensei. That's often forgotten. Not by everybody, but by many people.

Etiquette during practice is that if you're better than the other person, you don't manhandle them, you try to train them. But you also don't make a baby out of them or cater to them. You push the area they need help with so they will learn and begin to understand. That's a good instructor.

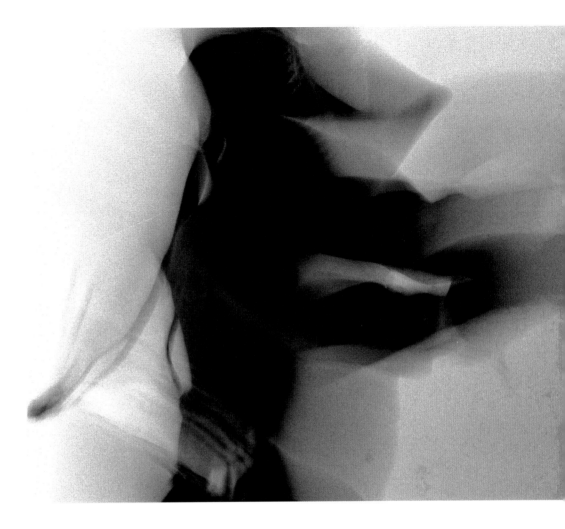

I welcome the student that has respect, even students that don't belong to our dojo that visit, as long as they respect the dojo and respect the sensei—which most of them do. I'm glad. Something is left yet of tradition and respect. Whoever comes, I take them. Like today, we had one Muslim girl ask to practice kendo. But she said she couldn't call me a teacher, because in the

I tell my students not to try to be too good right away, not to be overly ambitious.

Muslim world, there's only one teacher—that's Allah. I said, "That's fine, just respect me, that's all I ask. Learn my teaching. You don't have to bow to me." Then she was quite happy.

I love kids that enjoy kendo. They don't necessarily have to be good. I mean, I hope they are good, but the main thing is that they enjoy it. I've had many really skillful students, and all they wanted was to be good. But after they stopped winning tournaments and other people started clobbering them, they quit. On the other hand, here's old flunky that can't do anything right, but he'll come and really enjoy kendo and get stronger in the end. It may take him a little longer. What normally takes three years might take him five years, but it doesn't matter, he's having fun. There are too many students concerned with winning or losing.

I tell my students not to try to be too good right away, not to be overly ambitious. Kendo is not ten easy lessons, it's years of practice. And if you enjoy it, you'll get good. Even if your guts are falling out because you're so tired, you can appreciate the practice, the sweating, the camaraderie. You pick up your friend and go to kendo practice, and then sit back and have a drink and just talk about it—there's a closeness. In kendo, you should always remember the people that did kendo with you, even though they may have quit.

Instructors need to be compassionate—to give hard love. It's difficult to be compassionate at times, because your patience is tested. But the best way is to make the kid enjoy what they are doing, not just focus on making them better. But there are limits. This is not a playground, not a social club. There are times you have to be harsh. As I say, you have to push them a little more, push them a little more—but not so hard they just can't stand it. Most of the kids now are coming not because their father sent them, but because they like it, so they may quit. Times are different. You have to help them have fun while they improve. That's where a good instructor has to test each student, because each student is different. You can't teach everybody the same way in a mass teaching, like in a gymnasium. You have to take them one at a time.

It's very important to find the right teacher. Like anything else, if you start off badly, you waste a lot of time. Just like going to a school that's not accredited. You might spend four years at a college, then find out you can't enter another university because that college isn't recognized. So you have to search. But

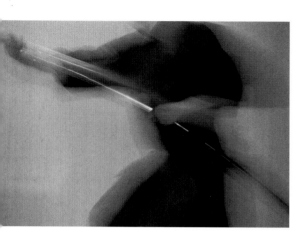

it's very difficult to ask, "Are you the right teacher? What are your qualifications?"

We recently had a student join here. He'd been to several teachers who taught how to draw the sword and that sort of thing, but then he saw me teaching how to hold the sword—fingering. Right from the beginning, before anyone even touches a sword, I teach them how to hold it. That's why this student joined my dojo. He said he had searched all over and finally decided on here.

But I don't know how you would ask a teacher about their credentials. You can't always ask other people either, they may not want to tell you the honest truth, perhaps they're friends with the instructor. It's very difficult.

Kendo is slowly losing its tradition—the old kendo way. The style done today is full of odd techniques, totally unacceptable by traditional standards. In the old kendo way, you don't guard yourself, you don't sit there all covered up. In other words, you throw yourself at your opponent regardless of whether you're going to get killed. That is a type of *waza*—technique. You don't throw yourself heedlessly into an attack, but neither do you guard yourself in order to sneak in a strike. Modern kendo has turned into win-or-lose kendo, even in Japan, and that will eventually destroy it. The psychology has really changed.

I'm not saying winning isn't important, because that's what

kendo is about. But how did you win? Did you win with funny movements or with the proper spirit? Did you win with a *waza* that was totally unorthodox and say, "Well, it worked, didn't it"? Is that a good *waza*? You must win, yes, but how? That's the hard part.

Years ago, when my kid was *shodan*, he won first place hitting *kote*, which is the easiest, most defensive tactic. You don't have to throw yourself. You don't open yourself to your opponent to take *kote*. So I told him he only won by *kote*. If he won by *men*, that would have been different. When you go for the *men*, you're totally open. Your *kote* will be taken, your *do* will be taken, you have to totally throw yourself at the mercy of your opponent to take *men*. That is a superior point.

What happened next tournament? He took all *men*; he began to understand. It's just like a matador throwing himself toward a bull. The horns might brush his side, missing him by just an inch, but he doesn't protect himself, he's wide open.

In a match, you need to have a free mind. All you have is your training. Your mind has to be clean. When either one of you attacks, that is the moment of truth. Yes, you can sit and watch for weak points in your opponent during other matches. And then, when your turn comes, you can keep that knowledge, not in the forefront of your mind, because he'll know right away what you're after, but on the back burner, ready for the opportune time. But it's not a guarantee. You don't know what I'm thinking, I don't know what you're thinking, and you may not be thinking at all—that's hard. So you test each other.

On the lower echelon, you can sense right away the feeling of your opponent. This guy's wild—you don't know what he's going to do. And this guy's sneaky—he'll try to fool you. But the quiet one, the truly good one, just does pure kendo and doesn't try to fool you. He'll take you one step at a time. Then when you do something—bang!—he'll come in. It's impossible to say there's really a true connection between each other, but you could say it's a feeling, it's a silent message, and it becomes quite intriguing. You know what he's going to do, but he doesn't do it, because he knows that you know, so he resists. He'll suck you in, in other words. And if you take the bait, he'll get you.

I did kendo with a person who was officially blind. His glasses were very thick. When he took them off, he couldn't see five feet, yet he did really good kendo. All he knew was feeling. He couldn't see you eye to eye, he could just see your shape, just feel you moving, and he would get you. So seeing too much is no good. You have to observe the person's total motion.

I can still do the physical part of kendo, but not for as long as I used to. It's hard to accept your own limitations as you get older, but I do—sometimes! The ones that don't accept have problems. I'll do the best I can, to my limit, but I will not feel defeated. Those are the two important things: to do my best and to not get frustrated. If a guy's good, he's good. I used to get frustrated. As I got older, the students started getting better and better—which should make me happy. Some teachers can't take that. They cannot take their students getting better, but that's what you are teaching for. So they lose sight of their goal. Sometimes I get frustrated because I can't do what I want to do with a student anymore. But I have to accept that too.

In my work in advertising, I would sometimes get frustrated because a client would tell me a concept was wrong or because of political hassles in the company. But you begin to weather that, you know, somehow you weather it. You understand, this too will pass . . . try your best. There are times I wanted to quit, but I kept at it, I believed there would be better days. Whether you're in business or not, I guess you could say kendo makes you a fighter. Not a bully. Perhaps a silent fighter. Kendo puts you in a place where you are really persistent.

Probably on the last day of my life I'll know what kendo's greatest lesson has been for me. I don't know now because I'm still doing it, because I am still learning. I'm declining, but still learning what kendo is. All my senseis that have passed away probably had different reasons, learned different lessons. But

I don't know, because I'm still enjoying it. If you enjoy it, you don't know.

Kendo has to be a part of your life, it is not something you practice. It's the same as religion. Kendo is religion, *budo* is religion. It's not something you dilly-dally with, practice and go home. It's part of your life. That's what kendo is, and iaido. All martial arts should become that way, part of your life.

You'd be surprised how many Caucasians can't speak Japanese or anything but begin to really understand. So you can't say, "Oh, you're Caucasian, you don't understand anything." Even the Japanese don't understand *budo*. Even the Japanese in Japan don't understand it. They talk about it. Well, you can talk about heaven and hell, but do you really understand? You don't. Same as *budo*. You talk about it, how precious it is and all that, but how many people really understand?

Here's one way Buddhism and kendo are similar. There's a word used often in the martial arts—*mushin*. It means "no mind." Well, in Buddhism, you help people, you do good things with no mind. You don't expect to get anything back. I'm not a practicing Buddhist in the sense that I go to church. But I practice Buddhism every day through my way of living. Even just sitting here, and the way I take my food. The Buddhist way is compassion, understanding. So I try to live in a Buddhist world. But I don't preach. To me, the

Probably on the last day of my life I'll know what kendo's greatest lesson has been for me.

whole thing is Buddhist. A fish in a little fishbowl doesn't know it's in a bowl. So although a person in Japan doesn't necessarily practice Buddhism, they live in it. In America, when you greet, you say, "How do you do?" and the response is, "Oh, fine, thank you." The Japanese say, "*Okagesama,*"—because of you, I am fine. See the difference? Because of my acquaintance with you, I am fine. It is a Buddhist idea. They greet that way all the time but don't know that it's Buddhist. They live in a fishbowl.

You don't know how long I've been doing kendo and losing money. The *bogu* I use was given to me because my own was so dilapidated. I don't make any money. And that's why. If I start making money, then I'll start getting greedy and then . . . well . . . it's not *mushin*.

Tatsuo Suzuki

Professor Tatsuo Suzuki was born on April 27, 1928, in Yokohama and graduated with a degree in economics from the University of Japan. He began training in karate at the age of fourteen, receiving direct instruction from the founder of Wado-Ryu karate, Hironori Ohtsuka, from 1945 to 1956. In 1951, he was awarded fifth-degree black belt—the highest rank in Wado-Ryu at that time—at the age of twenty-four.

After moving to England in January 1965, Suzuki founded the first Wado-Ryu karate federation in the United Kingdom and it quickly spread throughout Europe. At the age of forty-five, Suzuki's accomplishments led the International Budo Federation to award him the master title of *hanshi*. Today, over forty member countries in Europe, Asia and the Americas comprise the Wado International Karate-do Federation (WIKF), established by Suzuki in 1991 in an effort to preserve the essence of Wado-Ryu karate.

Suzuki sensei holds black belt ranks in Tenshin Koryo Bo-Jutsu and judo, in addition to his eighth-degree black belt in karate-do.

I MET OHTSUKA SENSEI after the last world war at the Wado
headquarters in Tokyo. He was about fifty. At that time, Ohtsuka
sensei was not only teaching but training with us. During *kata*,
he would be right there among us. His speech was very gentle,
but his spirit was very strong, like a real samurai, so I respected
him very much. He was so wonderful, technically and mentally, it
was always my ambition to be better than him. I never compared
myself to anyone else, only sensei. I thought of him as a father
and he treated me like his son.

I would train with Ohtsuka every day. Once, when he was
about sixty years old and I had just graduated from university,
I came to class in very bad weather. I was the only student there.
O-sensei always told me to relax, because my shoulders were too
tense. My karate was very powerful, but not relaxed, which he
didn't like—Wado is a mixture of relaxation and sharpness. He
would say to me, "Your shoulders are too hard, too stiff. Relax."
I knew it mentally, but physically I couldn't do it. So on the day
when just the two of us were in the dojo, he taught me a basic
jodan zuki, and I did it again and again, up and down and up and
down the floor for two hours. Just that one technique. I began

very tense and punched as hard as I could. But soon I got tired and, naturally, relaxed. After that, I understood a little better than before how to relax my shoulders.

But O-sensei was always very good to me. For example, he used to belong to the International Martial Arts Federation. He was the top man for the karate section. One day he said to me, "I want to interest you in getting *hanshi* from the International Martial Arts Federation." I said to him, "No, it's too much for me." Because at that time nobody—only O-sensei—nobody in Japan, no Japanese instructors were *hanshi*. But one day he gave me a certificate and a silver cup from the president of the federation—who was the emperor's uncle—naming me *hanshi*. Ohtsuka sensei paid for everything, so I couldn't refuse.

Another time when I was a university student, fifth dan was the highest grade. I was a third dan already and thought that was enough. But many other students pushed me to test for fourth. "If you cannot take fourth dan, we cannot take any dan," they would say. I said, "No, no," but finally I decided to test for fourth dan. I remember that grading at Tokyo University—it's one of the top schools. When it was finished, O-sensei said to me I was a fifth dan, not a fourth dan. I said, "No, no, sensei, please give me fourth dan—it's enough," because fifth dan is the top. Only two or three other students were fifth dan and they were forty or fifty years old. I was a university student. So I said, "No, this is too much. Please, give me a fourth dan." But he said, "All the examiners agree you are a fifth dan, so you must take it." So I took it, but nervously.

I just wanted to train hard. I don't even remember when I took first dan or second dan, even third dan, because I wasn't interested—I just trained. I never thought about dan grades. Only my fifth dan test I remember because of what happened.

So now I tell students, "You must train hard. Dan grading is not so important." But Westerners always think about what dan they are. This is wrong. I want to tell them—I want to show them. I am still training. Somebody asks me, "When will you retire?" When will I retire? When I am dead. They ask me why I keep training. They think I am good enough—perfect. This is a stupid question. I must do many things. I must continue to practice all the time. Of course I have not practiced enough. Even if I practiced only one punch all my life, it would not be enough. People think after twenty, twenty-five, thirty years of age, their training is finished. This is not martial arts. Martial arts is a lifelong pursuit. People say, "Oh, I'm too old, I can't train," but this is wrong. It doesn't matter if you are forty, fifty, because karate is not only physical training. If you train with spirit, you can start at any age. One of my students in England started at fifty-five years old. He died about five years ago at seventy-four or seventy-five. He became fifth dan and taught every day at five clubs. And just before he died—his wife told me—he stood up and performed *kata*. He did four or five *kata*, then passed away. His spirit was very strong.

About ten years ago, I went to China to watch Chinese martial artists. Every day for two weeks, morning and afternoon, we would talk and share techniques. They all agreed that fighting is just one side of martial arts training, not all. But nowadays, in many countries, karate is only practiced for the fighting. This is wrong. People just want to fight in contests—they're all about thirty years old. Before thirty years of age, a human being has lots of stamina. But after thirty, every year stamina goes down. Even with hard training, stamina goes down. But if mental training is included with physical training—if the spirit is trained—any age can improve. This is important. But it's not done and it's absolutely wrong. Karate is a martial art, not a sport. This is important. Nowadays people only think of

sport karate—I don't want to be a part of that. What is important is the spirit, not the technique.

For example, when I was a university student, I often went to meditation. Zen meditation, with Genpo Yamamoto and Soyen Nakagawa. The training was very hard. At that time, I was training karate ten hours a day—everybody said Mr. Suzuki is crazy—and

after karate, I would go to Zen training. Occasionally there were special courses called *seishin* that lasted a full week. All day, we would just sit down and meditate. One hour *seiza*, five minutes *keien*. Then again. From four o'clock in the morning until midnight—all day. It was very, very hard—harder than karate. I never knew anything so hard. This, though, is very useful for martial arts. It's like the idea of *fudoshin*. *Fudoshin* means to always remain calm, never say anything. Then, even if a great rock comes down from the sky and crushes your body, it cannot crush your spirit. This is *fudoshin*.

There is a story about the famous swordsman Musashi Miyamoto. One day, he met a general and told him he had seen in his ranks a very good samurai, a true samurai. The general asked who it was and Miyamoto sensei described him. So the general called the samurai into the room. Musashi Miyamoto told him, "Your general wants you to commit seppuku. Right now." The samurai's face didn't change, he just said, "Yes, sir," and prepared. Musashi said, "Stop. I must ask you. What special training have you done?" "No special training," the samurai replied, "but one thing. Every evening, when I'm in bed, a *katana* hangs on a tiny string from the ceiling just above my throat." In the beginning, the samurai couldn't sleep because he was afraid. But soon he accepted the *katana* above him and he slept very well. Musashi Miyamoto nodded and said, "Yes, that's why you're never afraid."

There is another story about a famous martial artist called Yagyu Sekishusai. He taught that the most important thing in the martial arts was to have a brave heart. For example, in kendo, bamboo is used for training. If you are hit, nothing happens. But with a real sword, just a touch will cut, so the feeling is different. With a real sword, one mistake means you might die. It's life or death, so there's real fear. But if you develop a brave heart, dojo training and a real fight have the same feeling. This is very important, but most people, if they were in a real sword fight, would move differently because they are afraid.

When students come to my dojo, we shout or sometimes hit their hips—it's a different atmosphere. So when they come to

If you develop a brave heart, dojo training and a real fight have the same feeling.

train, their mannerism is absolutely different—changed. Parents are very surprised by it. If they practice long, they are changed, slowly, slowly. This is important. In the beginning, they don't like the severity. But if they stay a long time, they will change slowly. Then many things—walking, personality—will also change. When the spirit is trained and made strong, it affects all of their person. This is good for human life.

Partners must respect each other. If an opponent hits me, I always think, "Oh, he's warning me. My block is weak, or my body movement is too small, so that's why he hit me. Thank you." This is important—respect is important. Nowadays people get upset and hit back.

One of our dojo *kun* is *jojitsu ni oberezu*. It means that instructors and students are not the same. Even if you are friends outside the dojo, inside the dojo is different. There is a manner to keep. You must train seriously. I tell my students, "*Ichigo ichi e.*" This term comes from the Japanese tea ceremony, but it is important to the martial arts also. It means that just now you are with your instructor. The instructor may die tomorrow, or the student may have to move on. So always think, this may be the last time you receive instruction. Watch carefully, train hard, because this may be the last time, these may be the final instructions.

Keiko Fukuda

JUDO

Keiko Fukuda was born on April 12, 1913, in Tokyo. She is the granddaughter of Fukuda Hachinosuke, who taught jujutsu to Jigoro Kano, the founder of judo and the Kodokan Judo Institute. At Kano's personal request, Fukuda began training in the women's section of the Kodokan, the Joshi-Bu, in 1935, and immigrated to Oakland, California.

After holding a fifth-degree black belt for nearly thirty years, she broke through the traditional ceiling of women's ranking in judo and attained the sixth degree in 1972. The year after, Fukuda sensei published *Born for the Mat: A Kodokan Text for Women*. In 1982, she became chief technical advisor for the United States Judo Federation (USJF) Kata Development Committee and, in 1985, a faculty member of the USJF National Teachers Institute and technical advisor of the USJF's women's judo division. In May of 1990, Fukuda sensei received the Medal of Honor—the Order of the Sacred Treasure, Gold Rays with Rosette—from the government of Japan.

The highest-ranking woman judoka in the world, Fukuda received her ninth-degree black belt on April 23, 2001. In recognition of this achievement, the city of San Francisco declared Keiko Fukuda Day on August 19, 2001.

I DIDN'T KNOW ANYTHING about judo. I thought it was just for men—I'd never heard of women taking it in Japan at that time. My grandfather was Kano sensei's first jujutsu instructor. After my father died, Kano sensei asked me to join the women's section at the Kodokan. Since my grandfather had done jujutsu, I thought maybe I would try it, so I began training for first-degree black belt. I went to the Kodokan every day from three to six o'clock for evening practice. I kept thinking, "When am I going to get black belt?" It took a long time! But after first dan, second dan came pretty quickly, and at third dan I became an assistant teacher. I thought I didn't have the knowledge to teach, but I had students, so maybe I did.

Kano sensei told us we would be going to other parts of the world to teach judo, so many of my classmates began to study English. They were all upper class, from the same circle as Kano sensei's granddaughter, who was also a teacher. I was there because of my special relationship to Kano sensei through my grandfather, so all the high-dan senseis were very kind to me. I was very lucky that way.

My father died when I was in second grade at private school.

After that, I changed completely. I studied very, very hard and graduated head of the class. That part of my personality carried over into judo too. Once an aikido sensei came to the Kodokan and everyone studied a little aikido—it's very interesting. But my mind never changed from judo; it was all I thought about. I think it's because maybe I have a part of my grandfather deep inside me. That's why I have taken judo all my life. I was never interested in studying naginata or anything else. My mind has only followed one path, straight—judo. It has proved very good for me, because I have studied judo deeply, and its important points I understand very well.

My mother wanted me to keep Fukuda, my grandfather's name, if I married. The women's name can often be used in Japanese marriages, so my mother asked Kano sensei if there was a judo-ka, a nice instructor, who might want to marry me. Eventually, it was all arranged. But then I realized that I would have to give up judo. Women instructors weren't allowed to marry—their class times were in the evening, when they were supposed to be at home preparing dinner—so I turned down the arrangement. My mind was already made up to teach in other countries. Very few women walked away from arranged marriages, but I had a strong mind. Several times after that people proposed to me, but I could never think of marriage, I just wanted to study judo. I found it more interesting.

Nowadays, men and women do the same judo. But their bodies are completely different. I don't like it. Women are using too much strength. It makes me worry about the future. I want to see more *ju*. Good judo, good technique—that is *ju*. Inside, *ju* must be working instead of strength. Women's bodies must be allowed to fit judo. When I was younger, I trained with tenth-degree instructors—their judo was so nice. The movement was good, smooth, like dancing. You wouldn't even know the sensei was throwing you. There'd be a little movement, then suddenly, "Oh, I'm being thrown." Now I don't see that kind of movement. Too much strength is being used, and I think a lot of girls get injured because of it.

We need good judo to come back, but I don't think younger girls know what that is. There aren't enough women instructors. So change will be very difficult. And at my age, there's not too

An instructor needs patience, which is why we have to have love.

much of a future, not a lot of time left for me to help. The problem is that judo is being taught the same way to men and women. I think my dojo is the only one in America just for women. Most dojos have only a few girls. It's difficult for women to practice with the men—there are too many injuries. I think more women would take judo if it was taught in a way that fit women's bodies by emphasizing technique, speed and spirit rather than relying primarily on physical strength.

I think a lot of people misunderstand judo because they only see the competition side. A few of the women are just interested in *shiai*—to be in the Olympics and international competitions. I don't force my students to go to *shiai*. Most of them are over thirty, and we don't send them after that. We have a few fourth degrees—they have good movement. That's what judo needs, and I think they have it. So they don't go to *shiai*, and that's fine, but judo still has to improve. I don't know how long the women's *shiai* will go on the way it is, relying on strength and with the kind of manners I see from some of the girls. Women's *shiai* is completely different now—we always kept good manners growing up.

My motto is, "Be gentle, kind and beautiful, yet firm and

strong both mentally and physically." It came out naturally from my heart—that's why people respond to it. I wrote those words a long time ago, but they still represent my life and I think they are very good to live by. Many other instructors ask their students to learn my motto. Of course, how much they understand depends on the person. I hope one or two students develop a real understanding of it and live their life that way; then I'd be happy.

I had studied judo for thirty years and I found out how important love is. The word in Japanese is *ai*. In Buddhism, love is the most important ideal. All religions are the same, Christianity too. There are many teachings, but in the end, they are all about love. So in my mind, I think, when I teach, I have to have love for my students. Because some of them are very easy to teach, but others take a long time to learn. Even with a lot of attention, it still takes them a long time. So an instructor needs patience, which is why we have to have love. There are many things about human beings I have studied through judo. That's why judo is not just a sport to me. I want my students to understand my experience, how I studied, how I was able to create my motto from my judo training. My students have to study hard and through their training also study these lessons for themselves.

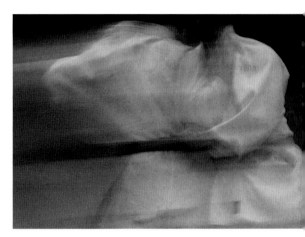

That is why manners are important. Without manners, there is no judo spirit. You have to be patient and study. You can't say,

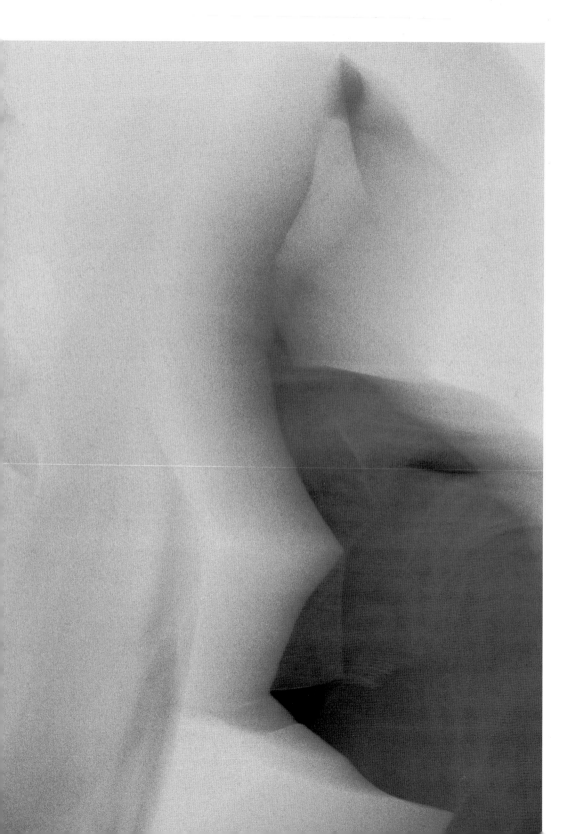

"Today I want to go to a movie, or dancing," or "I'm not feeling good." Then judo is absent and you never study. Whenever you don't feel good, go to the dojo and exercise, then you'll feel better and soon you'll be practicing. Patience is very important to judo. Judo makes very serious people, I feel—people with good manners, who would never talk too much during practice. Then, when students go to school, they behave the same way and do well in everything. That's real judo, I feel, when the instructor teaches it that way. I studied very seriously myself, three hours every day. My judo is not just sport judo—that's very important.

Students also need to study

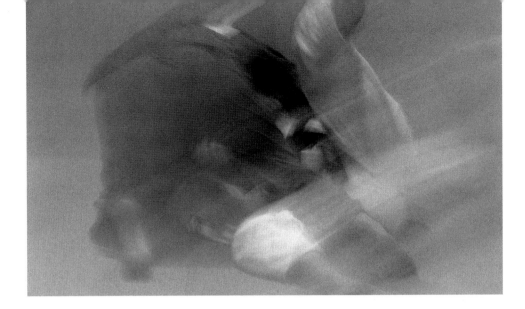

the Kodokan motto, *jita kyoei*, or "mutual benefit." I tell my students to help each other, to think of each other and be kind to each other. Don't think of always doing things your own way. Consider other people's ideas, find agreement. This will help you become a better person in everyday life in many ways. That's the way I studied judo.

My own senseis were sometimes not so kind when they criticized my technique and I would cry and cry, from one train station to the next all the way home. But I had patience. That's why I am here now, with the rank I have received. My friends that quit just needed a little more patience, that's all. You may meet other judo people that are a different type. But I have studied judo technique in a way that lets me study the way human beings ought to live. That's why judo has taught me so many good things. And I appreciate judo, Kano sensei and my grandfather for it.

Yoshimitsu Takeyasu

KENDO

Yoshimitsu Takeyasu was born on December 2, 1920, and began his career in kendo at the age of eight. He graduated from the engineering department of Tokyo Imperial University in 1941, and was appointed to a senior government post as Deputy Secretary of Japan's Science and Technology Agency in 1973.

In 1976, he became chairman of the Research Development Corporation of Japan, and fourteen years later, he became president of the Japan Resources Association, a post he still holds. In 1991, Takeyasu sensei was decorated with the Order of the Rising Sun, Gold and Silver Star, and since 1997, he has been the acting chairman of the All Japan Kendo Federation.

KENDO IS NOT A SIMPLE PART OF MY LIFE. I have never lived without kendo in the past forty years. I've become involved with the administrative side of kendo, and at the same time, I have continued my practice. My energy, vitality and physical strength have all been enhanced by doing kendo. It helps me work with vigor and it has strengthened my willpower. I have developed an unyielding spirit and try to live in society with a sense of righteousness. You can win at kendo technically, skillfully, using technique, but that is only a one-time thing. Eventually, the final goal is to find the right method of living—to go through life the right way.

Individuals each have different reasons, different purposes for studying kendo. One may be practicing kendo to become an instructor, to be involved with educating students—they need special training for that. A good teacher is one who can teach kendo with the whole personality—not only skill and techniques—but the heart and soul of it. A good teacher is one who can set an example for others. However, the teacher must still be accomplished and able to demonstrate. Another thing that is important is that the teacher shouldn't teach too much. They should only assist or guide the student to advance by themselves. Less teaching is better.

If a teacher is really good and is the right one for you, then you should remain with that teacher. But it's very hard to find a really good instructor, so you may want to try others. This applies only to the beginning or early stages of training. Once you have advanced to a certain level, you don't need any more teachers. You have to cultivate your understanding of kendo by yourself—it's not a thing you are taught. Kendo is not like other athletic sports where emphasis is placed on beating a time or a record. Kendo is not like that. You have to read your opponent. What is he going to do? You have to read your opponent's mind. In that sense, anybody can be a teacher.

To be a leader, you have to acquire the right method of teaching. Yes, teachers must be able to instruct correctly, but they also need to teach kendo in a way that excites students' interest, so you need leadership qualities to be a good teacher. There is a saying that you shouldn't copy teachers, you shouldn't do as the teacher does. You have to look at the attitude of the teacher, find out what the teacher is seeking, what the teacher is looking for. That's what the student has to grasp. Being strict just for its own sake is not a good thing, it must be significant to the students. Teachers must understand what level of intensity or strictness is needed.

Not all traditions are good but we have to identify the ones that should be kept. About two hundred years ago, *shinai* and

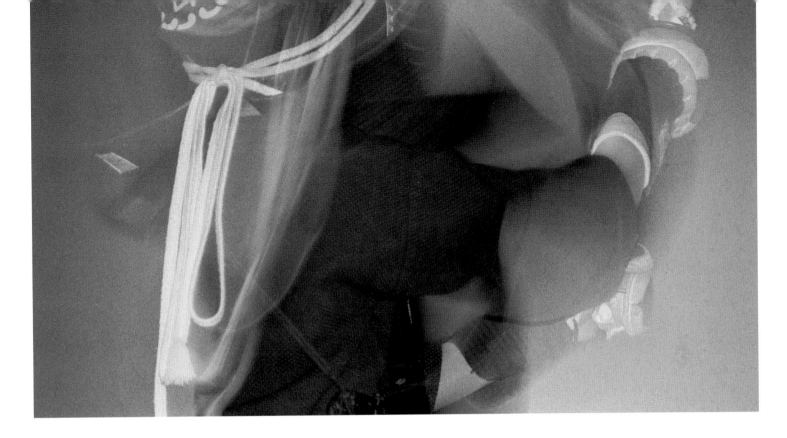

bogu were devised, and they were a wonderful invention. The formalization of kendo was made during that period and we are very proud of it as an ancient Japanese sport. In that sense, the history of kendo is not long, perhaps only two hundred and fifty years old. At one time, kendo went through a period of decay. However, around 1895, an organization was established in Japan to promote kendo. Unfortunately, Japan became involved in World War II, and after the war, when we were occupied by the Allied forces, using swords was considered a military activity. Kendo was misunderstood by the Allied forces, and it was officially banned. After the war, in 1952, a new organization was established,

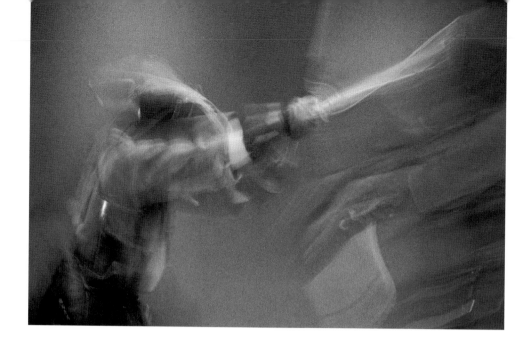

uniting all of kendo into the present federation. The federation celebrated its fiftieth anniversary in 2002.

We are attempting a new start for kendo in the twenty-first century. Our purpose for this year and for the future is to observe our traditions, but with a renewed spirit toward cultivating people through kendo. We hope many people throughout the world will become interested in kendo, and through training, they will become well balanced both mentally and physically and will be of service to society.

We're not, however, interested in becoming involved with the Olympics—they've become too tainted by commercialism. If they were authentic and observed the real Olympic spirit, we might reconsider. But, you know, those competitors train exclusively for the Olympic Games, and once their participation in the games is over, it's all finished for them. As far as kendo is concerned, training continues throughout your whole lifetime. Kendo is practiced differently depending on the age category of the practitioner, whether they are younger children, college students, people who are working or more elderly people. Kendo itself is different depending on how old you are.

The biggest difference from the kendo practiced in olden days is that more emphasis is placed on winning at matches. This is particularly apparent at schools. It can be said that kendo is a form of self-expression. Through practicing kendo, you can acquire fulfillment—it is an expression of yourself. So winning and losing is a secondary matter in that view. Kendo does have a sport element. However, if emphasis is placed on that element only, then I think it becomes negative. Of course, once a kendo match is started, you have to win, and the *shinai* and *bogu* protectors are the tools you use for that. But there are two aspects: the sport aspect, where winning and losing are still very important, and also the spiritual aspect of kendo, which is profound and highly valued.

A foundation of training in the basics is very important. The fundamentals must be learned continuously—that is the most important thing. Kendo should not be uniform. It has to fit the individual. So you should try to establish a form of kendo that is

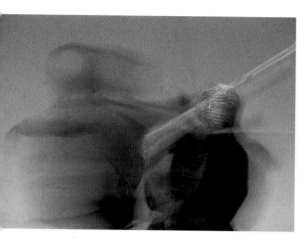

appropriate for yourself, not like someone else's. You have to exert yourself in pursuit of that. If you start when you're young, this may take you twenty years, so an early start certainly helps. Starting kendo at an early age is the ideal. However, if you begin later in life, you can certainly still benefit from it. There are a number of people who have reached quite advanced levels even though they started in the later part of their life. For example, one lady who started at the age of sixty was promoted to sixth dan.

Kendo has spread worldwide and women have started practicing, which was not the case in olden days, when kendo was practiced by a limited circle of people. Compared with the olden days, however, I feel the average skill level is lowering, and most of the emphasis is placed on competition, not on spiritual training. But as kendo-ka get older, this changes. These days, kendo is practiced well by older generations.

We use a *shinai* for practicing, but kendo is based on the use of a sword, so it's not a matter of hitting, it's a matter of cutting. That's the ideal—not to hit, but to cut. In order to do that, technique is required. Kendo is not the kind of thing you practice for only two or three years; you must continue throughout your life. And if you cannot, it is a loss, because your effort will be wasted.

Of course, to be the best kendo artist, having natural ability is the ideal. However, not many people do, so to grow as a person,

the spiritual aspect must take precedent. As I mentioned, kendo is
not something to be practiced for a short period of time—it has
deep meaning, profound significance that takes time to uncover.
With a substantial understanding of the basics, you should be able
to continue for a long period of time. Being a good sport about
losing, you should continue. If you cannot appreciate this
characteristic of kendo, you are not seeing its true benefits.

Mitsusuke Harada

Mitsusuke Harada was born on November 16, 1928, in Dairen, on the southern tip of Manchuria, but returned to his family's native home in Japan after the Soviets invaded the country of his birth in 1938. In 1943, at the age of fourteen, Harada took his first karate class at the Shotokan, built by master Gichin Funakoshi, the founder of Japanese karate, as the first dojo constructed expressly for karate in Japan. After the Shotokan was destroyed in a bombing raid in 1945, Harada began private classes with Funakoshi sensei.

During the 1950s, Harada became influenced by masters Shigeru Egami and Tadao Okuyama, and in 1956, he moved to Sao Paolo, Brazil, to work at the Bank of South America. Under Funakoshi's instruction, Harada organized the Karate-do Shotokan Brazileo, the first organization of its kind in South America, for which he was awarded his fifth-degree black belt at the age of twenty-eight.

Harada moved to Great Britain in 1963, becoming the first Japanese instructor to live there. Two years later, he formed the Karate-do Shotokai Organization.

AIKIDO, KENDO, JUDO—the martial arts all have much in common with one another. We respect each other. I have many good friends in the other arts. It's only the karate group that can't get along, even within the single style of Shotokan. They never speak. I'm friendly with maybe four instructors—all the other groups have never met with me. There's something wrong, don't you think, with this kind of a martial arts society? This in particular I don't like about karate. If you watch other sports, rugby, for instance, they are sportsmen, they respect each other. But in karate's case, I don't know.

Other people are aware of this about karate too. If I go to Japan, or if I meet a Japanese person who doesn't know me, naturally there are introductions, and right away they ask me what sort of work I do. As soon as I tell them I teach karate, their respect for me goes down. Honestly. It's nothing I have done, Japanese society just doesn't respect karate instructors. On my business cards, I don't mention what my profession is, because I'm ashamed.

Karate has a very low social standing in Europe too. Professional instructors—the ones who want to make money from karate—have no education, no personal career, they teach karate because they couldn't get an ordinary job. So the public perception of karate is very low.

What's worse are these instructors' egos. They have an inferiority complex that amounts to a kind of racism, a disrespect for anyone not of their nationality. How can these people teach *budo*? It's absolute nonsense. When I look at the group in karate, I don't see many gentlemen. And I often wonder why. Did karate itself create this type of personality? Or is it that this type of personality is attracted to karate? I think it's a bit of both.

On the other hand, my students are all professionals. One is a university professor who has created a dojo right in his house, just for his own practice. But no one recognizes this group. No one notices the people who practice karate just for its own sake. I'm very interested in this phenomenon.

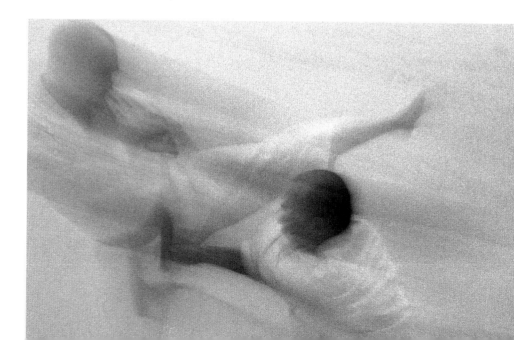

If I have one hundred students, for example, only ten or so will engage in competition. The other ninety aren't interested in medals; they are interested in *budo*, in learning the martial ways. So, in Japan, I raised the question of what to do with the 90 percent of people who don't compete, but no one was too interested. In fact, the impression I got was that no one was sincerely interested in karate at all.

In this sense, I deeply respect Funakoshi sensei—he never had those kinds of feelings. In religion, there is the notion of turning one's face to God. Well, exactly like that, he turned his face to karate. He was one in one hundred thousand. Completely devoted. Even in his eighties, when I used to pick him up every Saturday to go to practice, he was revved up, excited. "Let's go! Let's go!" he'd say. You know, I don't think Funakoshi sensei knew it himself, but the way he was, *that* is *budo*. No ambition except to practice.

Without developing relationships, friendships, you can't practice, especially in karate's case, because there is so much *kumite*—fighting. And if fighting is treated antagonistically, without respect for one another, you can't develop. We must learn from each other. For instance, the Japanese don't know European culture, and the Europeans don't know our Japanese culture, so we share with each other, find out which is wrong and which is

right, which is better or worse. Both cultures are thousands of years old, so we respect both sides. I learn about European culture, but I also explain about my own culture. This attitude of learning from each other and respecting each other must be applied to practice.

You can't teach martial arts, you've got to steal it—you've got to catch it. What I mean is that you need to practice with a partner. You must accept attacks, not just practice in the air by count. Every kick and every punch and every block is different. When you feel the variations in capability between partners, you begin to understand why you were able to catch one but not another. Bit by bit, you steal the knowledge of what is effective. But if instruction is all verbal, misunderstanding is inevitable. The point must be proved, demonstrated, felt, stolen. You've got to catch it.

Attitude is very important. If someone is not interested in real practice, if they're just along for the ride, they will never understand. You have to practice seriously. That's all. I've had a lot of experienced karate people complain to me that there are no black belts in their area, so they can't train. This is absolute nonsense. If you don't have any black belts, train some from beginners. Then you'll have lots in your area. Since I left Japan, more than forty years ago, I've hardly practiced with advanced groups at all. When I lived in Brazil, no one knew karate, so what my beginner students did, I did too. My group in Britain has been created in the same way—from the bottom up. I'm always asked, "Who is your instructor?" My students! They're my instructors, because we learn from each other.

For me to succeed, I must find the weaknesses in your technique. That's my philosophy of practice. Egami-san talked about [aikido founder] Ueshiba sensei's ability to throw people seemingly without touching them. He told me I must endeavor to produce this effect with my karate technique. And I believe I have succeeded. I call it *hakkei*, because I don't like the common word *kime*, "focus," which implies a stopping of power. *Hakkei* is more relaxed. It's hard to explain. Even if you are Japanese, it is difficult. The word originally comes from the Chinese, from tai chi, but their pronunciation is different. If I showed the lettering to a Chinese person, they would understand, but still, my concept is different, it is my own.

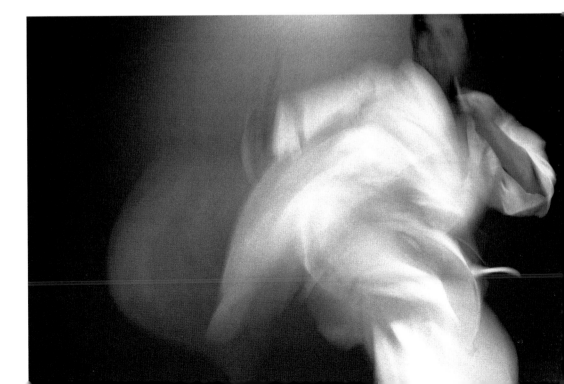

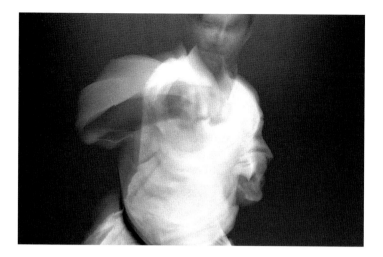

But you must understand, it requires a special technique. I don't want people coming from all over to test my claim. That would be dangerous; they or I could get hurt, or even the people watching. It's like professional baseball players. They can only hit a home run from certain pitches. Not anyone can pitch with the speed and accuracy required; it takes someone who knows what he is doing. I can produce the effect with my closest students, because their intentions are true.

Visualization during *kata*, during forms, is important. But your imagination must be based on your experience in *kumite*. That must come first. The relationship between the two is very important. It can't be fantasy. The point in *kata* is to learn how to apply the movements in reality, how to train the body to adapt to situations in a flexible way. The second purpose of *kata* is to train the muscles, to allow for the movement. Funakoshi sensei's method was to teach *kata* by counting. I can't say if his method is right or wrong; it was his idea. My idea is quite different. To me, counting the movements is gymnastics—fantasy. So I changed my method. We don't use counts to practice our *kata*.

Everything must be found out for yourself. For example, we can't accept the idea that karate is important just because someone tells us so. It might be for that person, but not for someone else until they feel it themselves. Therefore, each person must find out why karate is important for their own life. You can't be told.

In my life, I've had two regrets. If I denied it, I'd be lying. I regret that I didn't do what I wanted. When I was working at the bank in Sao Paolo, I told my boss that a friend was opening a dojo in Paris, and I asked whether I should quit the bank and try to become a karate instructor in France. Ninety-nine percent of the people at the bank thought I should stay. They told me I could become a manager or an executive in the future. So I almost stayed. But two people, my boss and another friend, said, "Harada, this is a very good opportunity. We can't go to Paris. You shouldn't miss out." So because of them, I made up my mind and went. That moment in 1960 I deeply regret. If I hadn't gone to Paris, I would have stayed at the bank. Now I have no retirement. I'm seventy years old and I can't carry on. If I'd stayed at the bank, I would have become a branch manager and retired in my fifties. This I deeply, seriously regret. I chose karate, and some parts of that decision I regret, but not karate itself. I have many friends in many different places around the world, and for that I am very happy.

The only other regret is that I never had a family, I never married. You know, with this job, marriage is impossible. If a woman really understood and supported what I did, okay, it would have been much better. But how many people would understand? I think only one woman in ten thousand would commit to marrying a person like me.

One thing I have learned myself. I'm a teacher, and I have taught exactly the same way in countries from Scandinavia to South Africa for nearly forty years, but the results have been different for each group. I teach them the same things, but each group turns out differently. Why? Naturally, because their backgrounds are different. So in the martial arts, in *budo*, we search for a truth, a spirit, a mental attitude. But this is something particular to Japan, to its history. In the case of Europeans, the knights of the Middle Ages, although not quite the same, were similar. In Britain, the idea of the gentlemen is close, but even this was developed from the Japanese idea. The concept cannot be duplicated exactly in other regions of the world; the results will always be different.

So it's ridiculous to ask which style of karate is better. It's absolute nonsense. We must practice with each other and learn from each other. I really respect Higaonna sensei for this. A student of mine attended one of his clinics and was using *age uke*—high block—to defend. He tried Higaonna sensei's method but wasn't successful, so he immediately changed to one of my ideas and he found it very easy. But this is normal. He had never practiced Higaonna's method and the way I taught him was what he knew best. When Higaonna sensei came over, he didn't say the technique was wrong or bad, he just asked the student where he came from. When he heard he was one of my students, he just said, "Ah, yes, okay." Because his idea is that style doesn't matter, what works is what's important—whether the student was able to defend himself. But most instructors ignore this. They think their style is the best, no matter if it works or not.

In the martial arts, in *budo*, we search for a truth, a spirit, a mental attitude.

Now, it's important to keep in mind that beginners and black belts are different. Until black belt, students must follow our method, to develop fundamental skills. Otherwise, they would only get confused. But after black belt, especially around second dan or third dan, the student has much more experience, and I expect them to travel, to experience other styles and other teachers. I want to give all the fish to the ocean—so they come back salmon.

Shozo Awazu

JUDO

Shozo Awazu was born in Kyoto on April 18, 1923. He began his lifelong training in judo in middle school at the age of ten and became a frequent competitor during his youth.

In 1948, as a result of his success in national competition in Japan, he was invited to France to coach the national judo team, a position he held for forty years. In 1963, then a sixth-degree black belt, Awazu authored *Méthode de Judo au Sol*, published by Éditions Chiron in France. In 1980, he was awarded the Ordre National du Mérite by the French government, and twenty years later, he was named Chevalier, the fifth-highest title of France's Légion d'Honneur, for his achievements in promoting sport in France. He currently holds the rank of ninth-degree black belt.

WHEN I WAS TEN YEARS OLD, I injured my foot and was attended to by a judo sensei. I was not big, but I looked quite healthy, I was strong for my age, so the sensei said, "Come to my dojo and I will teach you judo."

It was difficult for me because my teachers were very strict. In middle school, my sensei had a reputation as a very tough disciplinarian, but it was a good judo school. It was just a sport to me, but I won a lot of medals, so it was very attractive as an adolescent and I continued through high school.

I used to train two hours a day, in the afternoon from three until five o'clock. Every day, every week, every month—longer on Saturdays and Sundays. I couldn't stop. It was a good dojo we had, one half for judo and one half for kendo. It wasn't a sports hall used by other groups but was built specially for judo and kendo.

I studied and learned and practiced more and more until I got results. I was quite well known in the judo world, I suppose, so eventually I was called to Paris by the French Federation to coach the national team. So I became a teacher. I was twenty-seven years old—that was fifty years ago. I was very interested

in helping the French judo-ka progress.

I don't think you can say everyone naturally evolves into becoming a teacher; each has their own character. But whatever you do, if you want to learn or to teach—in Japanese, the term is *sen*, "teach"—if you want to progress, you must stay mindful of Kano sensei's principles, the Kodokan mottos *seiryoku zenyo* and *jita kyoei*.

The first notion, *seiryoku zenyo*, is efficiency—efficiency of the good energy. This is very important in Japan. Even if you're little—not very strong—you can win against someone who is taller or bigger. *Jita kyoei* is the idea of mutual prosperity. It means my training is not just for me, it's for us both. This is important to keep alive in judo. It is the notion of generosity to classmates, the spirit of learning, of giving. These were the principles Kano sensei founded judo on.

When your body is bent, it means your spirit is like that also.

Japanese writing is made of Chinese characters, each of which can be interpreted differently and given different meanings through their various combinations. One of the meanings of judo is the formation of character. Today most of the discipline and etiquette are not respected and the spirit of judo has been a little forgotten. It's not good. In judo, you must salute your seniors, follow the etiquette. This is important for all *budo*. In Japan, *do* is very important. And without the proper spirit, there is no *do*.

When I started judo, the training was much harder because of the constant repetition. It's something I don't sense now at the training camps. There's no deep work. It's superficial—for winning. There's less time spent on training—on repeating movements, gestures, positions—and more time spent on competition. It's regrettable. Now that judo is an international sport, different countries have introduced other techniques just for winning, for medals. They're not good, because they're not "straight," they're just for championships.

You must have straight posture, because that shows you have a straight spirit. If you are bent over, broken, it's defensive. It's not a straight position, it's not a straight spirit. When your body is bent, it means your spirit is like that also.

The straight line of judo has been a bit destroyed by these modifications from around the world. It's possible for judo to recover from this, but only when the techniques progress will judo progress. In Japan, there are, of course, Japanese teachers, but teachers are local in other regions of the world. It's possible they didn't perfect the origins of judo well enough to teach the basic straight line of judo, so perhaps it's the organization that has allowed these positions to damage the spirit of judo.

My interest now is to look after young people who are practicing judo. I want to contact them to help ensure they learn the straight way. In the future, I hope judo-ka will go back to the origins of judo and learn the techniques. It is one of the Ways. There are three fundamental functions: preparing, destabilizing and attacking. Until those three things have been learned, you cannot return to the origins of judo. They are the way back, both for individuals and for judo in general.

One of the most important things is natural movement. I would like to see young people relearn this. When you don't do natural movements, you become very tired. But by training, by repeating the actions yourself, natural movement arises and the understanding becomes deeper. It's like drawing. The first time is not so good, the second time is better. If you keep repeating, the gesture improves.

You must observe your opponents. If you have been trained well, you can see where their mistakes are and will be able to push your attack in this vein. But you must know a great deal about technique. If there are five pupils, my advice to each student will be different because their bodies and styles will be different. But with training, and *randori*, you can learn to recognize your own mistakes.

The best judo-ka can't be described within the context of competition, of winning or losing, but only as the one who does straight judo, natural judo. Mentally, too. They have a natural mind. The Japanese word is *mushin*. It's the notion of being pure,

simple, natural. If there is a single moment of reflection when you are attacked, it's too late. The thought cannot exist in your mind before performing the movement. It must be instinctual, without thought. With constant training, the movements become automatic, like a reflex. If you don't do judo like that, it's not judo.

Be kind to your pupils. Be kind and be generous—that's one thing I've learned. Kindness has been a line for me my whole life, and I have always been thanked for it. My own master, Yoshizawa sensei, was not kind in the formal sense, but he was so wonderful it produced a natural respect in me, and that is also a form of kindness.

Judo develops you as a person. You learn a spirit of attack and a spirit of defense. And it teaches you patience as you continually repeat the movements. The greatest lesson I have learned is the state of study, the state of difficult effort—spirit. Without judo, I would be much poorer.

Finally, *budo* is the difference between being quiet and not quiet. The whole idea of *budo* is a big problem with Westerners. You need to know the culture of ancient Japan to understand it. Historically, during the times of the samurai, *budo* was very important. Perhaps, as with competition today, it's not whether you win or lose, because in samurai times a battle may have been

won one day but lost another. So you can't be interested in that, but just in the fact of being quieter than your opponent. If you are quiet, you can see things very naturally and choose any strategy with serenity. This represents the path for the judo-ka. There is no end, no aim, no pinnacle to achieve. You can continue forever.

Hiroshi Tada

A I K I D O

Hiroshi Tada was born on December 14, 1929. On March 4, 1950, while completing a degree in law at Waseda University, he began studying aikido under the system's founder, Morihei Ueshiba. Seven years later, Tada received sixth dan, and in 1961, he established his own dojo in Jiyugaoka, Tokyo.

In 1964, he went to Italy to promote aikido, and subsequently established the Aikikai of Italy. He remained in Rome as a teacher until returning to Japan in 1971. In 1994, Tada was promoted to ninth degree, received a Distinguished Service Medal for his contribution to martial arts and became a committee member of the International Aikido Federation, a position he still holds today.

Tada sensei teaches regularly at the Aikikai headquarters, Waseda University and Tokyo University. He is also the chief instructor at the Aikikai of Italy and chairperson of the Tada-juku dojo.

I HAD HEARD OF AIKIDO while I was a child. Ueshiba sensei was very, very famous in Japan. He was a master teacher of many martial arts, including judo, kendo and others. He was considered a teacher of teachers. I knew his name since childhood, but because the war broke out, I couldn't join his dojo. After the war, I entered Waseda University and I heard his name mentioned again and was soon able to enter his dojo. At the time, I had no idea what aikido was like. I didn't know what any of the techniques were or anything at all about it. I just longed to meet Ueshiba sensei—he was greatly admired. All the students in the olden days were more or less in the same position, they all wanted to meet Ueshiba sensei. Back then, aikido techniques were not shown to the public; only the military and members of the royal family had any experience of it. So none of us had ever seen any techniques at all. To join the dojo, I needed recommendations from at least two people, but I was lucky enough to be accepted, and I found it was a wonderful, magnificent place.

My impression of Ueshiba sensei, when I first saw him, was that he had a sort of atmosphere about him, an aura surrounding him that filled the whole dojo. The impression was not only revealed in his technique. For example, in other martial arts, there is a confrontation between two combatants who stand in opposition to one another, and the one who has the stronger or better technique will win. However, in Ueshiba sensei's case, he transcended this confrontation. If he wanted to use his technique—any technique at all—he could do anything. But he never used one to crush his opponent. His techniques were never used for injuring others.

What I had learned from Ueshiba sensei and other wonderful teachers, and my interest in tradition, kept me doing aikido. The traditional way of practicing applies to modern society not as a matter of physical skill, but as a mental or spiritual technique. The basic idea is to transcend confrontation. In daily life, you may become angry or sad, or full of fear or hate, but those feelings arise out of a confrontation in your mind. You have to transcend that, you have to go beyond.

So what should you do? The answer to that is the supreme goal of the martial arts. Nowadays many college students practice martial arts, and of course, one of their goals is to build up their physical strength. But more important than that goal is what I have just mentioned—to transcend. And this is related to your level of concentration. The Asian technique of training is found in transcending confrontation. I will explain.

On one side we have the heart, the mind or heart, and on the other side physical objects, everything you see—the things that continually come into your mind. The Zen Buddhist Takuan said the same thing—he had the same philosophy. Your mind is occupied by objects, by things—this is ordinary life. But with this kind of mind, occupied by things, various feelings and emotions arise, which means that your mind is resting. However, if you observe things sharply or clearly, using your mind as a mirror, then your mind keeps its composure and is tranquil. This is concentration of mind. This is *keichu*. *Keichu* translates as "concentration," but the general interpretation is not real concentration, in my experience. This state of mind can be attained through practice—it is called Zen. In Sanskrit, it is called *dharma-dhya*. *Dhya* refers to a state of mind that is interpreted as Zen in Japanese.

Now, why is this required in martial arts? As I said before, anger, fear, sorrow, envy or hatred—all remain in the mind as things. In traditional Japanese martial arts, emphasis was placed on the mind being able to see clearly, on removing these objects that would keep the mind resting. But recently this has become very difficult because the martial arts are becoming a kind of sport. So there isn't much emphasis placed on this kind of concentration. It takes a long time to learn these ideas, this

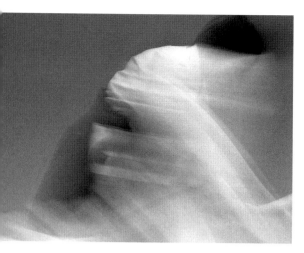

system of practicing, and in sport you cannot afford to spend your time so abstractly. In aikido, we don't have any competition for just this reason. If an unskilled person competes, he will try hard not to be beaten, not to be thrown or to try to win, and those will be the habits gradually developed.

So the sport aspect is going in the opposite direction from the traditional way of doing martial arts, and this is the biggest problem facing the martial arts world. What should we do to go beyond confrontation, what sort of method should we utilize? This is what must be sought in this century. You will know when you get older. For example, suppose a person is sick, is suffering from some kind of illness. Is it good for that person to fight against this illness, or is it better to coexist with it, to increase the body's natural healing ability by keeping peace of mind? This is the same in martial arts, because in this state of mind, the mind is always free. It is not bound at all, not occupied by things.

So we want to preserve aikido as a traditional Japanese art. But to do this, you have to know the system, the mechanism needed to attain the supreme goal of the Way. If you take the opposite approach, naturally it's very difficult to reach. Training methods are the same as transportation systems. Suppose you want to go Kyoto. Well, you should get on the Tokaido line or the bullet train. If you get on the wrong train, then you will be taken to the wrong place. So you have to find out what your purpose is, and how you're going to achieve it.

After the Meiji era, Yukichi Fukuzawa advocated Japan's disassociation with Asia in favor of European ideas to promote modernization. In some senses, that approach was a success, for example, scientific research or the military system. However, from the philosophical point of the view, the loss was great. The martial artists of the modern day are not informed about this system, or mechanism. I happened to be very lucky to have met Ueshiba sensei, who observed the traditional side of martial arts, and thanks to his and other senseis' teachings, I could get to know them. Japanese people have the tendency to see things from the point of view of an overall impression. They don't look into the specific mechanism of study or research; they're more concerned with generalities, with appearances. But more emphasis should be placed on a practical form of practice. As I said before, the way to reach the supreme goal of the Way requires a specific mechanism. And this mechanism already exists—it was discovered two thousand years ago.

Many of the traditional ways of practicing were introduced along with Buddhism and Confucianism. But it's difficult today to teach within the framework of religion. So traditional ideas need to be taught with a modern interpretation or, as much as possible, a scientific rationale. The way of practicing shouldn't be too difficult or too complicated, because then people cannot follow it. It has to be gradual, step by step. You have to pay attention to your state of mind when practicing techniques. Whatever your mind hopes or wishes, your body will move toward, even if it is only at the subconscious level. For example, in the martial arts, we call it *mushin*, "no mind." Without any thought, the body will move by itself. That was what Tempu sensei [founder of Shin Shin Toitsu Do] taught. The body and mind are bridged through nerve functions. The training of this is also very important. In a yoga sutra written two thousand years ago, there were eight laws described that detailed what a person should or shouldn't do—not to kill, not to steal and so on—but the basic concept underlying all of them was the way to keep a peaceful state of mind.

So this is the first step of training. After you've trained your mind, then the physical training follows. For example, breathing as we practice it is different from the Western interpretation of breathing. We are taught scientifically that oxygen is breathed in and carbon dioxide is breathed out—that is the mechanics we are taught at school. However, Eastern breathing techniques are not limited to that explanation. We receive *ki*, or energy, from space. We are living in the energy of space. *Ki*—or *prana*, which is the Indian word used in yoga—is absolute energy. *Ki* is the absolute force where all energy originates—it makes existence in this world possible. So we can receive this absolute energy through a special method of breathing and take it into our body. In this way, the human body can be said to be like a battery. Human beings are creatures of the Earth, but at the same time, we are creatures of space. As creatures of the Earth, we breathe in oxygen. But as creatures of space, we receive this absolute energy

force. In the East, human beings are considered a microcosm of the larger macrocosm of the universe. The Japanese tradition is fundamentally based upon this way of thinking. So the method used when breathing is to control your senses, like the tactile sense, for instance. There are many senses of touch—the sense of movement, the sense of pressure, the sense of pain—and all these senses are divided into smaller subcategories. For the control of those senses, *budo* is the best. Suppose someone grabs your arm. You observe the attacker carefully. You can feel the attack, you understand it, so your mind is very calm and keeps composure. So through training, we can control our feelings, and if you can do that, you can enter the stage of true martial arts.

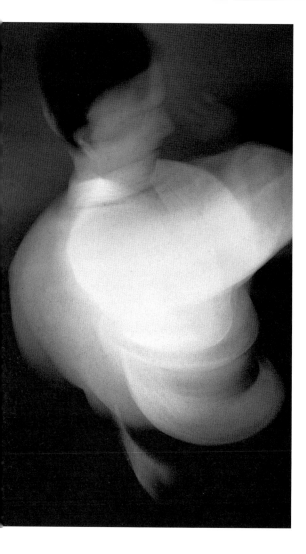

The force, the unseen force which moves this world, and our relationship with it, is very important, and very important for our future too. Ueshiba sensei said that you must love your opponent. This is because the foundation of space is love. Without love, nothing material could ever be created—not so much as an atomic particle could be combined. Love makes all evolution and advancement possible. Why does such a law of space exist? It is probably because progress and advancement had been repeatedly made in space itself and human beings had also progressed with it.

So this ability, or capability, should not be abused for enmity or the destruction of the world. Japanese martial arts originated on the battlefield, under the idea of kill or be killed. But through true training, you will attain a peaceful mind and understand *budo* is not a tool to be used for such things. When you understand the rules given from space, you understand that these excellent rules should not be used for devastation or violence. We have to transcend that.

The people who discovered this had practiced martial arts from childhood, had trained at shrines or deep in the mountains. They found a new way. Ueshiba sensei was the same. He is the founder of a martial art, not a sport. People like him are yogis. Yogis who are also samurai—very spiritual. However, in these modern times, the competitive aspect has been emphasized and the spiritual essence is weakening and becoming lost. Only the physical aspect of building up outward strength is being researched scientifically. This is the tendency in recent years. There are only a few people who are researching the spiritual aspect of the martial arts. As I said, a specific training method is needed, but unfortunately it's missing these days, the original research has been excluded.

So this is our problem, how to restore, how to get back to the original way of practicing. It is a critical time now. This century is the beginning of a new era. While competitive sport is important, coexistence, the training of coexistence, will become more important. But it cannot be done in a hurry, in one day or in a short time. It takes a whole life—and must be done very quietly.

In the ancient martial arts book written by Seizan Matsuura, it is written like this: "The dojo is the dressing room of the theater." Daily life is the real stage. In the dressing room, you can prepare, you can hear advice from your seniors, you can learn and make corrections. You cannot do these things on the real stage. This was said about three hundred years ago.

> It takes a whole life—and must be done very quietly.

Shigeru Uchiyama
SHORINJI KEMPO

Shigeru Uchiyama was born on December 15, 1917. After studying judo as a young boy and later teaching judo to various police forces, he encountered a demonstration of Shorinji Kempo and immediately began to study the system with its founder, Doshin So, in 1952. By 1971, Uchiyama had been conferred the title of *dai-hanshi*, and in 1982, he was decorated with the Distinguished Service Medal. In 1992, Uchiyama was awarded ninth degree. Five years later, in 1997, he was honored as a distinguished instructor on the occasion of Shorinji Kempo's fiftieth anniversary.

The government of Japan honored Uchiyama again in 1998 with the Order of the Sacred Treasure, Gold and Silver Rays. Uchiyama sensei is an executive board member of the Nippon Budokan, executive director of the Japan Martial Arts Council and an executive board member of the Shorinji Kempo Federation.

He currently resides in Tokyo and is the world's oldest living exponent of Shorinji Kempo.

IN MY OWN CASE, if I had lived only for myself, I would never have made the progress that I have. I have kept to the idea that mutual improvement comes first, and thanks to that teaching, I have had a very happy life. I am very lucky that I got to know Shorinji Kempo, and I want to disseminate its ideas to as many people as possible. The people who take these ideas to heart will have an enjoyable life even once they are retired.

In a match, the winner is not in any sense better. All practitioners are human beings. To strengthen your heart or technique, you have to get along with your partner—you must work for mutual enhancement. If someone acquires higher technique and then becomes strong, he may be proud of that. But from the viewpoint of Shorinji Kempo, it's different. We believe in living half of your life for yourself and half for others. So to attain your goals, to improve or cultivate a better personality or to work toward a better world, you have to work together with your partner. If you acquire a certain technique, you may boast. But as a human being, how to respect others, how to get along with others, is the technique you have to learn. Of course, physical technique is also important, because Shorinji Kempo is self-defense. In order not to be beaten, you have to acquire technique, but it has nothing to do with winning over your partner. The founder said he didn't practice Shorinji Kempo to become technically strong. From the beginning, this is what I found was different about Shorinji Kempo—it is part asceticism.

I have been practicing Shorinji Kempo for fifty years—the founder taught me directly. When I first got to know about it, I was very surprised by this idea of improving yourself and your partner simultaneously. It's not a matter of beating the opponent—the technique itself is very significant, it has a very deep side to it. Winning or losing is not the primary concern, the idea is to build up your body and spirit together with your partner. I was very impressed by the value placed on human life, and the idea of cultivating yourself and your partner mutually. The religious aspect of Shorinji Kempo also attracted me. Before I got to know Shorinji Kempo, I had done other martial arts and still lived in the world of winning and losing. I was amazed by the asceticism of the religious school of Shorinji Kempo.

We practice Kongo Zen, a form of Zen Buddhism. It's very hard to understand, even for Japanese people. The symbol of our incorporated foundation is a Buddhist symbol. It represents the universe and is composed of opposite poles: heaven and earth, positive and negative, male and female. These opposites keep the universe in balance. It symbolizes our way of thinking, and that of Japanese Buddhism. We call it *dharma*. Dharma is the force of the universe, which is our object of worship. *Dharma* is a Sanskrit word for truth, and it encompasses the basic philosophy of Shorinji Kempo.

There are four incorporated branches of Shorinji Kempo, but none is stressed above the others because they all follow the same truth. Besides, their functions are totally different from one another. The religious corporation teaches techniques based upon religious ideas of Shorinji Kempo—that is their function—the incorporated foundation promotes Shorinji Kempo and

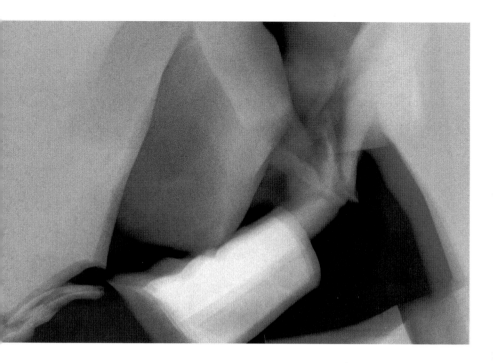

disseminates its ideas, the incorporated school educates the teachers, and the world organization unites and governs all of Shorinji Kempo. So all four corporations have their own functions, but they all follow one truth.

We have six basic expressions that sum up the characteristics of Shorinji Kempo. *Ken Zen ichinyo* is the first. *Ken* symbolizes the body, although the literal meaning is "fist." *Zen* comes from Zen Buddhism and represents the mind. The saying means that the body and the mind, although they seem separate, are actually one thing. It doesn't have any meaning to only train your body, you have to train your mind as well; otherwise, your mission will not be performed.

Riki ai funi means love and strength are not two things. They sit in opposition to one another, but they are not separate—both are needed for harmony. A person who has strength but is not tempered by love is not a full human being. Also, love can only be properly given and protected with strength.

Goju ittai expresses the necessity to unite the hard with the soft. And so hard and soft techniques are combined in Shorinji Kempo.

Fusatsu katsujin means to not kill others but let others live. Shorinji Kempo is not intended to beat others by hurting them. We have to cultivate our skill for mutual improvement, to let others live as well without harm—that's *fusatsu katsujin*.

Kumite shutai means that technique will always be improved by working with a partner.

Shushu koju is defend first and attack second. The prime idea is self-defense. So all techniques of Shorinji Kempo are forms of self-protection; they are not offensive.

Up to this day, I have been working to pass down correct Shorinji Kempo to the next generation and have remained faithful to its truths and philosophies. That is what teachers should keep in mind. All my pupils—the ones that haven't died—are still teachers. Many martial artists develop their own styles, in karate or aikido, for example, but as far as Shorinji Kempo is concerned, there is only one school—it's not possible for students to establish their own. So we have no intention, no idea at all to create another school of Shorinji Kempo. Because of that, we instructors must understand the teachings deeply and know how to convey the ideas of the founder correctly.

The teacher who can transmit the truth or essence to the next generation—that is a good teacher. The one who can hand down the teachings correctly and who works hard for that purpose.

Practitioners are not obligated to teach—they can make their own choices. But at the same time, if someone is very good and they keep that inside and won't share their talent, that is not a good thing. Shorinji Kempo has grown because the techniques and the way of thinking are very deep and precious, so it became popular quite naturally.

I try to teach beginners to improve themselves and to contribute to world peace. To be strong means to be strong against yourself, not against other people. Many people with weak minds commit suicide—we have seen many cases of it in Japan. Those people have been hurt, their minds are weak, they are not strong. But you *have* to live strong. You have to become a person who is a positive influence on others. Some people make wishes, or rely on other people, or pray to God. No, you have to exert your own effort to improve. And improving yourself means that you consider others. If you take this idea into yourself, problems will not arise.

I came up to Tokyo to practice and to teach Shorinji Kempo. Before that, I was a public servant in Kanagawa prefecture. While I was there, I became the vice-chairman of the Prefectural Worker's Union. Recently, a case of corruption by an executive member of Jichiro, All Japan Prefectural and Municipal Workers' Union, has been disclosed. Although he happened to be a top member of the union, he didn't know the nature of things. There are many people who pretend that they know the principle of things but actually don't. I'm teaching Shorinji Kempo because I want people to understand principles through Shorinji Kempo. All problems arise when emphasis is placed on making profit, on

making money. When you try to be good for others, good for society, then these sorts of problems won't come up. When Shorinji Kempo is practiced, we need a partner, and together with this partner we improve, we try to motivate one another to work for others. So I tried hard to disseminate Shorinji Kempo to the workers at my municipal office.

In working life, you might make a profit or you might end up losing money. Some people who have lost heavily may commit suicide or do the wrong thing. But knowing how a human being should be—that's a very important thing. By trying to bring about mutual happiness, you will create a better society and improve your own situation. This is very important. As far as business is

Live every moment with all your energy. Don't stop, keep going, steadily—that is life.

concerned, you have to make money, but sometimes you lose money, and people's lives are often ruined by it. Even if you are working at a business office, if the president of the company has this way of thinking in mind, then he will strive to bring the employees a happier and easier life. If you live only for yourself, you will not last, you will not survive. You have to change the way you live— yourself. And if you can keep this idea of mutual happiness to the very end of your life, then it will bring you great joy.

Some people who are looking for a better salary may switch jobs because they are only interested in profit and money. But by continuing what you started until the end, you will win eventually. I feel that strongly. The people who complain can never be satisfied by anything. If an offer for 10,000 yen better pay comes from another company, they will switch. Okay, so they can move, but their mind is always occupied by that way of thinking. People who are always looking for easier work experience the same thing, and life becomes very barren for them. Even if they are not well paid, people can work hard at a job to make the company better, so whatever the salary, they can

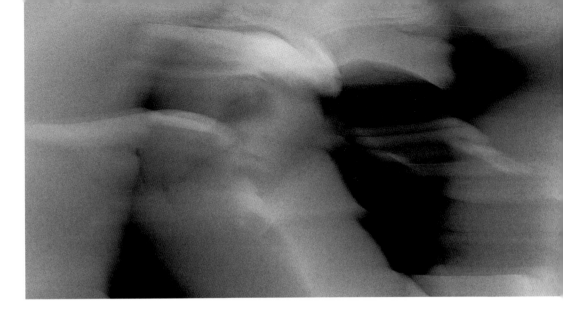

still find value in working there. People who are always thinking about making more never appreciate what they have. When you've eaten a good meal and you're full, you cannot eat any more, no matter how beautiful or delicious the meal is that is served. That can be said about everything.

If your life is already decided, you cannot change it. I am eighty-four years old. It may already be decided that I will die at the age of eighty-five. I don't know the situation—that's why I continue to strive. You have to work hard to the very end of the day—this is what makes life worth living, what brings you happiness. I may die tomorrow. If I work hard until the very end of my days, that's a good life. You don't have to be intimidated by death, it will come anyway. So I try, I give the utmost effort. You don't have to be in fear. Live every moment with all your energy. Don't stop, keep going, steadily—that is life. In that sense, I was very lucky that I could encounter Shorinji Kempo. It taught me how to live.

Rod Nobuto Omoto

K E N D O

Rod Nobuto Omoto was born in Wahiawa, on the Hawaiian island of Oahu, on September 9, 1918. He began his training in kendo as a school boy at the Wahiawa Hongwanji Japanese School, inspired by the sword play of popular *chambara* movies. In September of 1938, at the rank of *nidan*, he was sent to Kyoto to begin his studies at the Budo Senmon Gakko, a national training school for professional kendo teachers in Japan—located at the famous Butokuden training hall. While there, he was a direct student and personal *uchideshi* of kendo *hanshi*, tenth dan Kinnosuke Ogawa.

During the war, Omoto was enlisted in the Japanese army, then, during the occupation of Japan, worked for the American forces as a translator.

In 1960, Omoto returned to the United States and earned an engineering degree from Oregon State University, then moved to Tacoma, Washington, where he became the charter president of the Washington State Kendo Federation, currently known as the Pacific Northwest Kendo Federation. He holds the rank of *kyoshi*.

I LEARN KENDO BY NOT LEARNING KENDO. Everything you do is kendo, even cleaning a room. Each swing, each strike, each walk you take, listening to what's happening outside, seeing from the back of your head—that's all kendo.

Kenji Miura sensei, my first sensei, saw I was getting pretty good, so he spoke to my dad and said I should go to Japan after high school graduation to learn kendo professionally. I went to Kyoto, to Ogawa sensei's dojo. He was a tenth dan at the time. I stayed there for four years. Ogawa sensei didn't teach me any kendo. I cleaned the house, polished the *tokonoma*, walked the dog, did babysitting, raised the *suzumushi*—it was just like being a servant.

In Japan, there are three national treasures: One is a sword, one is a jewel and one is a mirror. If I think in terms of kendo, the mirror is to reflect yourself. You know, before you shave, you look ugly in the mirror, so it helps you make yourself look nice. If you are weak, the mirror will say you are weak, you've got to be stronger. After you really go into this—forging and tempering your physical strength, your mental strength, your *hara* strength, the soul—everything about you becomes stronger. But you're not polished yet. You've got to polish yourself until you become a jewel. It's just like putting yourself in a rock tumbler. Nobody's teaching each other, but everybody's in the rock tumbler, becoming a jewel. Why? Because of the *ken*. Because of the sword. The sword is not a weapon, it's just something I can build on, something I can use to create life. With this sword, I'm going to temper and forge myself and polish myself so that I become the same quality as this sword. It's not a weapon, it's a work of art. So that's the goal. That's my whole life.

A good instructor is the one that doesn't teach. I use the term "kendo dummy." I'm just a kendo dummy, trying to help the other guy improve. I don't have to improve, because I have the mirror to improve. Naito Takaharu didn't consider himself a sensei either. He was a great man, the greatest sensei I know, the first sensei of the Budo Senmon Gakko—the professional kendo school. When his grandfather found out that his son's wife was pregnant, he took her to the dojo to listen to the *shinai* and the shouting, and he gave her kendo books to read. So although Naito Takaharu sensei lived to be ninety-eight years old, he was involved in kendo for ninety-nine because he was being educated before he was born.

Anyway, he didn't keep strict rules, he didn't say people had to do this or that. He allowed people to do whatever they wanted, and if they were going in one direction, he could steer them back in another direction.

Tradition is not important. If you say tradition is important, you have to act according to that. You're forcing yourself. You don't do things because you love it—you've got to go by your tradition. Bullshit. What's the big deal about? I'm just trying to share my kendo experiences. I'm not a sensei, I don't teach kendo, I don't have the quality to teach kendo. Ogawa sensei, just like the other great senseis, didn't teach me any kendo. I just watched and learned myself. So actually I don't have any students, I'm not a teacher, I don't teach them anything.

When my wife was sick, this place was turned into a nursing home with twenty-four-hour care with hospice people looking after her. I watched what they did and thought to myself that I could do better than that. So I told them they didn't have to come anymore and I took care of her from then on—for four years. I quit my job, everything, until she died. You know, not an ordinary man can do that. This is kendo. Daily life. My life is kendo.

See, "kendo" is not important. It's just what became of my lifestyle. Everything I do is kendo. They call it *inochi gake*—put your life on the line. Everything I do is with my life on the line. I'm just trying to get ready to die, to leave this place. One of the Buddhist teachings says that I have entered this life, and I must appreciate that. But I'm going to terminate this body that did kendo and go to another, be born to another life, and I'm preparing for the transition. I'm reading religious teachings over and over again, and I'm convincing myself, convincing myself. I'm living my life from the kitchen to this room.

There are only four things we do in our life. You do the same four things. You go to bed, you get up, you eat and you move. Those are the only four things you do, for the rest of your life. You go to bed. You go to bed, you get up. When you get up, you have to eat. And then you move. Do your work, whatever, that's moving. Only four things.

So that's what I do, eat, move, go to bed, get up, eat, move. That's the repetition for the rest of my life. So I'm ready to die. And just before I do, I'll say, "Oh, I don't want to die"—I'm a human being. But a kendo-ka says, "I'm going to die with a peaceful mind," and all that. No, that's bullshit. When I die, I'm going to die, and that's not under my control. And I'm prepared to die, from way back.

I'm trying to fade away, not become a great sensei. I want to write my biography for my kids. My brother-in-law died in Beijing and he had nothing—no will, no history, nobody knew about his life. I want my daughters to know what I believe and to know that I did kendo, so I'm writing. I'm practicing for the end of my life.

I started thinking about dying and wrote out my thoughts on my computer so my kids won't have any problems.

Weakening by the day, but still doing my daily activities without putting burden on others.

There's nothing wrong with preparing to die. In fact, it's better to prepare than not to prepare.

Why think about dying? I will die because I was born.

I will never be completely ready for death, no matter how well I prepare.

*But the thing is to live until I die, live fully, and enjoy life while
living. And take care of my health, both physical and mental.*

*Because I do not know when I am going to die, or where, or under
what circumstances. I have no choice whatsoever. I will have to accept it
when the time comes . . .*

A school teaches how to kill, a dojo teaches how to die.

This is the kendo life: "Without burden to others." When I
become a burden to others, I want to fade away. That's what I'm
preparing for, preparing to die. So I tell my daughter, when I'm
no longer capable of doing housework, cooking, shopping, mail,
my computer work, then I'll go to her place. I'm not going to a
nursing home. I'll go to her place and stay there. She's already
got my room, my bed, half of my clothes there.

To me, kendo and death have no relationship. I cannot hear so
well, I cannot see well, I cannot eat well, but kendo is something
that's in me, that gives me the drive to go on—nothing to do with
death. Yukio Mishima—he's a renowned writer—is the last one that
did the formal seppuku. In kendo, you're not supposed to commit
suicide. But in the olden days, if you did something wrong, you had
to—to apologize. But now there's nothing to apologize for.
Committing suicide is against my way of thinking of kendo. Live as
long as you can, like Takaharu sensei—ninety-eight. Live as long as

you can to be of service to the community. That's kendo. That's what I'm preparing for.

I keep Buddhist teachings hung on the wall in the kitchen and out here. So when I eat, I look at them; when I work, I look at them. Back and forth. Kitchen to here.

> Those things that don't make common sense are the ones that really mean something to me.

Tannisho (*Lamentation on Deviations*) is another really good teaching that makes sense to me. "Everybody goes to heaven. Even the good guys go to heaven." Western thinking says heaven is up there and hell is down there. Yeah, good guys are supposed to be going to heaven—that makes sense. But in Tannisho, it says *even* the good guys go to heaven, and you may ask, what about the bad guys? The bad guys have already given up going to heaven, so they are free, they are already up in heaven. So those things that don't make common sense are the ones that really mean something to me.

There are two types of people who practice kendo. One is the curious type. They come in and they quit, because they know the whole thing already. They learn *men*, *kote*, *do*, *tsuki*. "That's it? Oh, I can do that." Knowledge. They stop at knowledge. But if they keep on pounding that knowledge, it becomes an art. "Aha, now it's an art." Some people quit there. They know the form and the art. But some people will keep on going, keep on pounding and pounding. And then Musashi Miyamoto's *ku*—it just disappears. You can't quit, because it becomes you. Everything in kendo becomes you. If it were taken away, you couldn't live. That's how I am.

Budo is "the way of *bu*." *Bu* means "arrow" or "spear," made from the symbols for "weapon" and "stop." So *budo* means "stop weapon way." That could be taken many different ways. If you have a weapon and you are trying to kill me, I block and stop you. But to me, in kendo, it's not a matter of defending against an outside attack. I must stop *myself* from damaging others. That's *budo*. My whole spirit now is not to damage, not to hurt others. I would quit kendo if it meant hurting others, if it couldn't be of service.

Mori Torao sensei, I think everyone knows him. He came from Japan and became a fencing coach in the U.S. He was the best kendo man in the whole world as far as sport fencing is concerned. He was really good. I met him first in Hawaii, and I fell in love with his form. I met him next in Steveston, British Columbia. I used to go there every year to judge and do demonstrations and be a kendo dummy for the people there. But at that time, he performed and my wife was really impressed. "Oh, he doesn't do kendo," she said, "he's just holding a *shinai*

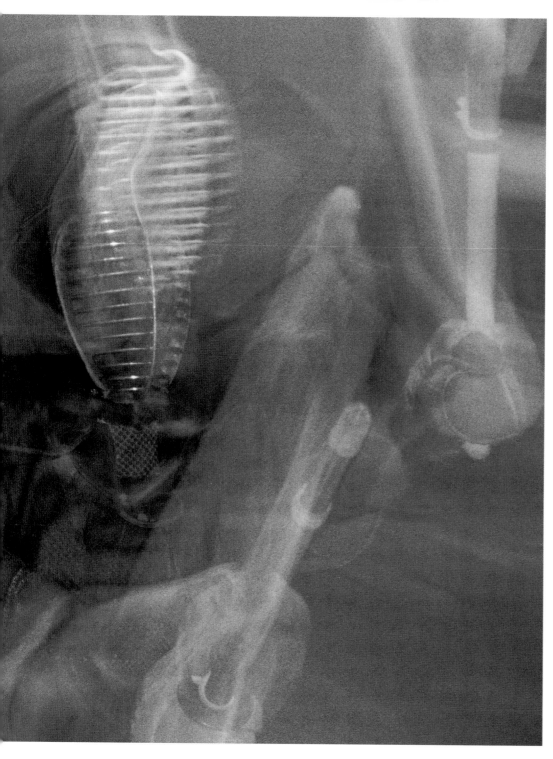

and dancing, and everybody's falling apart."

There's no bragging. The great ones never brag—Torao, Ogawa, Musashi, Takaharu—but the performance is so great that other people say, "Wow!" That's what it is. In other sports, there's all kinds of gestures and posing and jumping up and down. Kendo has no emotion. If you show your emotion, you lose. If they show emotion—boom!—all you've got to do is hit. You just be calm. When they get angry—tap—that's it.

So when you do *shiai*, relax and see the other guy move. Encourage him to hit you wherever you want him to hit, then say, "Hit now, this way, hit my *men* now!" Then he'll be on your terms. Don't play his game. Stay calm. When you're in *shiai*, keep two thoughts: One, beat the other guy; two, don't get beat by the other guy. Do your practice every day, every day, and then when you go to *shiai*, forget about it. When you're on the mat, you'll have already been conditioned. You cannot do better than what you did in the dojo, no matter how hard you try, no matter what you think—you can't do it. So let go.

I often quote Miyamoto Musashi, "A thousand *keiko* is just to forge and temper. Ten thousand *keiko* is to polish what you forged." I repeat it to everybody. I repeat it to myself. A thousand *keiko*. A thousand-day *keiko*. So I describe that to myself—a thousand days—and think about it. I ask people, "How many times do you practice?" Usually once, only a couple of hours at the most. So now count a thousand weeks. How many weeks in a year? Only fifty-two—if you go every week. And a thousand-day *keiko* is just to forge and temper. So you better be going for another fifteen years!

Forge and temper, forge and temper—that's my advice. I don't say, when you hit *kote*, do this way and do that. No, that's just knowledge. My advice is for you to become better, not me. In order for you to become better, one thousand *keiko*. Just be at the dojo one thousand times and see what happens. You will become a sensei.

Toshiro Daigo

JUDO

Toshiro Daigo was born on January 2, 1926. He graduated from Tokyo Higher Normal School for teachers in 1947 and became a professor at Japan's National Police Academy in 1966.

His career in judo began as a young boy, and by the age of twenty-six, he had won the All Japan Judo Championships in 1951, a feat he duplicated again in 1954. In 1976, he managed Japan's first Olympic judo team at the twenty-first Olympic Games in Montreal and received a Distinguished Service Medal for his contribution to sport. Three years later, he became a councilor at the Japan Sports Association. Daigo sensei was a member of the Foreign Minister's Sports Exchange Subcommittee in 1983 and again managed Japan's Olympic judo team in Los Angeles the following year. In 1985, he acted as the chief of the general education department of the National Police Academy, and in 1986 he was decorated with a Distinguished Service Medal for his contributions to the police force.

Since 1986, Daigo had been the chief of the instruction department of the Kodokan and from 1990 until the present an advisor to the All Nippon Judo Federation. He currently holds the rank of ninth degree.

MY LIFE ITSELF IS JUDO. Without judo, I wouldn't exist, and I will continue it until the very end of my life. Even now, every morning I come here to the dojo at 5:30 in the morning for practice. When I was young, I started judo at the very beginning of every morning, not necessarily by practicing in the dojo, though. While I was walking along the street and looking at the feet of passersby, I would think how I could sweep their legs. I was educated in that sort of atmosphere and just took it for granted. But to young Japanese people, judo becomes judo when you put on your judo costume. So without the costume, judo doesn't exist. It's a very strong tendency among the present generation.

Judo requires effort and time to master; it's a very, very hard thing to achieve. Once you begin, it takes a great deal of time. The same can be said of other sports, but, first of all, the student must like judo itself and must be committed to it. Without genuine enthusiasm toward judo, you cannot be good at it. Many students today don't consider judo a lifelong pursuit. To them, it's something they can say they've practiced, just another kind of experience. Compared with other sports, judo is very conservative, not flashy, and nowadays that's what young people

are looking for. So the younger generation isn't too interested in judo. They're going to other sports, and as a result, the judo population is declining, unfortunately.

Judo has a very wide variety of techniques, and teachers must acquire a deep understanding of all of them. Competitors today have acquired only a limited range of techniques, just what's needed to win. My teacher, Takagi Hajime, was marvelous. He understood a wide range of techniques very deeply, and so I was able to discover my favorites. Too many teachers have a limited range, and so can't lead each student to the techniques most appropriate for them. But if the teacher has acquired a wide range of techniques, he can see which junior student has the possibility of becoming a good judo-ka.

The Japanese tradition is for the teacher to place the student in very hard circumstances, not to teach easily. The teacher requires the student to learn by himself. For instance, tactics can be taught to students, but at the same time they must be different, because they depend on the person practicing. Individuals have to learn a tactic and then form it in their own way so the tactics can become their own. This requires the student to make a great deal of effort. The teacher has to be strict, but has to know the reason for being strict. Teachers, like students, are full of energy and passion, and some teachers occasionally exceed the limits and are rough with their students. But they don't do it because they hate their students, they do it out of love, out of affection. So as a student, I was beaten often.

It can be said about other sports too, but judo is not just play; it's a lot of pain, a lot of suffering. With spirit, effort and determination, you become patient and so become very useful to society. Mr. Keita Goto, an early disciple of Jigoro Kano shihan's, established one of Japan's biggest companies, Tokyu. He was very famous in Japan, and he said that what he learned from Kano was to never be defeated, to never be discouraged, not under any conditions. You have to just keep going on and on toward your target. On many, many occasions, we will feel defeated or discouraged, but we must have *nanikuso*. *Nanikuso* is a Japanese word for "spirit." My life itself is judo, my spirit is dedicated to judo, so whatever circumstances arise, I won't be defeated. But Kano was a very strong-minded man. I am not. I sometimes feel that I want to give up. But I expect at times that can be said about anybody, it's only human.

Judo requires a partner. You cannot pursue it by yourself, you always need an opponent so that you can both become strong together. In ancient times, when warriors confronted each other on the battlefield, they identified who they were, gave their name and the name of the lord they were subject of; it was all very fair. Only after the mention of their names and their positions would they begin their duel. This was a tradition among the samurai; they respected their opponent, and it remains a tradition still in the martial arts of Japan.

So you need that spirit when you practice. With that spirit, you can establish very close, intimate relationships. Without it, you cannot be said to be a human being, you are an animal. Kano shihan said that winning is the purpose, and in striving toward that final purpose, all human aspects must be formed, achieved, so you can develop harmonious relationships in society. That is the aim, the target to strive for. So it's not selfish; you have to become better, as well as your opponent.

It's really important when you start judo to study correctly with a good teacher. You need a very stable foundation. And you have to set your targets further in the distance than just winning matches. When you become an adult and are mature, you have to place your target far beyond, into the distance. When I started judo in my childhood, I just set my sights on

winning matches, just a few months or years ahead. But that's not good.

You have to utilize judo's physical, mental and spiritual aspects to the fullest, and in order to do that you have to acquire technique. This was one of Kano shihan's philosophies. He said through your practice, you and your opponent must prosper together. Now, when I was younger, I didn't consider, I didn't see these deeper aspects of judo, I just I wanted to win. My purpose was very short-sighted. But after a lot of effort spent training and after my career in competition, this spirit came into me and changed my way of thinking. When I teach, I try to educate people to become helpful to society, to contribute. This is my ideal. I cannot be the same as Kano shihan, my effort is very small, but I am trying my best.

Many people cannot excel in judo, even though they practice a lot, because they lack ability. But the fact that they have made a

lot of effort means a great deal. The winner in the match is not always the winner in life. So although they lack ability, making an effort is still significant. There are people who have won a lot of medals who have been losers. Judo players have a very short competitive life, so it's natural, when they get old and cannot compete, that they should use their experience to lead a better life.

When Kano shihan established the Kodokan, he placed the emphasis of judo on throwing, because it defeats the opponent completely. A person who is thrown receives a shock equivalent to ten or fifteen times their weight. We insure our safety by mastering *ukemi*. Then we practice on top of tatami, and also the Kodokan has a sprung floor, so the shock is absorbed. Although the players are thrown down very physically, they are protected, it's not very dangerous. But if somebody who had never practiced judo was thrown on the street, he'd be killed. This is the martial aspect handed down from jujutsu.

> We have to keep the fire he began. It will be difficult, but this is my mission.

The word *ippon* means to defeat the opponent completely so he cannot recover. However, in competition judo, winning is the final goal. So if a player cannot take *ippon*, he will try to win with small points; winning is winning either way. In my time, we had to take *ippon*, but youngsters think that winning is all there is, so they only try for smaller scores because they can still lead to a win. This has changed judo itself. Competitors break the rules, or pretend that their opponent has, to try and take advantage of the match itself. They'll also try, when the judge isn't looking, to hurt the opponent. Today you can come first place, be a gold medalist, without ever taking *ippon*. It's become a sport, and only about winning.

It will be very, very difficult to bring back traditional judo, but we have to. In particular, the people of the Kodokan can't give up; we have to preserve judo as it was handed down from the founder, Kano shihan. We have to keep the fire he began. It

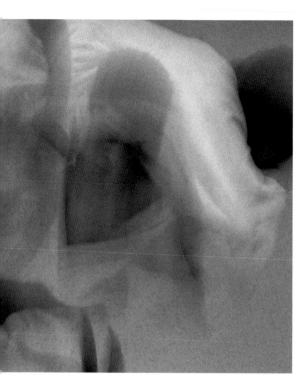

will be difficult, but this is my mission. Although it's not a very large number, a few of the younger generation do share the same opinion and aren't concerned only with winning, so there's a possibility the fire will stay lit. I'm trying very hard to teach them, but once my generation is gone, it will be very difficult.

When the Seoul Olympics were held, I was the manager of Japan's judo team. We were defeated, we only won one gold medal, and I quit, I resigned at that time. There was a lot of discussion about what route Japanese judo should take. The Japanese method of judo is to take *ippon*. But the judo practiced in foreign countries was focused on competing, on winning, so the methodology was different. The Koreans focused mostly on becoming physically big, on building up their competitors. But the Europeans focused on practicing techniques that win matches. So it's possible Japan was behind in this regard, and the result was only one gold medal. The Seoul Olympics were held in 1988, and afterwards we discussed it a lot. We were faced with three choices: to continue going after *ippon*, to build up the bodies of our competitors or to rely on tactics to win matches. After a lot of discussion, we decided that if we gave up taking *ippon* and concentrated on building up the body, our Japanese players wouldn't be able to win the gold medals, so we should keep to the traditional way of taking *ippon*. From this base, we practiced

new techniques and building the body structure. We looked for
opportunities to have as many matches with foreign opponents
as possible to see what we could learn and to see what sort of
techniques they used. But in the end, Japan continued to win gold
medals in the Olympics because of the decision to use techniques
for taking *ippon*.

When we lost in Seoul, all the commentators said Japanese
judo was finished. Judo established by Kano shihan must be handed
down from generation to generation. This is important, but
winning is important as well. The Japanese players are marvelous,
they're very sharp, have very sharp techniques. The audiences
in foreign countries are all attracted by the Japanese style of
winning. The foreign method of piling up small scores, it's not
very interesting, so the sport itself becomes dull. If the Japanese
players use the techniques of *ippon*, as well as the other, smaller
techniques used to pile up scores, audiences in foreign countries
will be very attracted to our method of winning by throwing *ippon*.
Then, once foreign players recognize the marvelous Japanese style
of judo, they will adopt the same route we are taking. So our
conclusion after the Seoul defeat was to keep traditional, to
demonstrate traditional Japanese judo. As long as we show
traditional skill and take *ippon*, Japanese judo will be okay.

Masami Tsuruoka

KARATE-DO

Masami Tsuruoka was born in 1929 in Cumberland, British Columbia. In 1945, he moved with his family to Kumamoto, Japan, where he began to study Chito-Ryu karate with the founder of the system, Dr. Tsuyoshi Chitose. By 1956, having attained the rank of second-degree black belt, he returned to Canada, where he opened Canada's first karate school in 1957.

In 1962, Chitose sensei appointed Tsuruoka the chief representative of Chito-Ryu in North America. The following year, Tsuruoka organized the first karate tournament in Canadian history. In 1964, he co-founded Canada's National Karate Association, and he was awarded the Centennial Medal of Honour in 1967. In 2000, Tsuruoka sensei was awarded the Order of Ontario.

Considered "the father of Canadian karate," Tsuruoka now teaches his own style of traditional karate, incorporating aspects of both the Shotokan and Chito-Ryu styles, and resides in Toronto, Ontario. He currently holds the rank of ninth degree.

YOU MUST UNDERSTAND that everything is a phase. Just like the body changes, what I believe will change. At one time, I tried to make champions. In Japan, I would never watch the old masters, I would watch the high school competitors. They were clean. Clean techniques. Clean minds. When they would lose, they would just lose. The old ones always cheated just a little. I was young then. My students were young. But I'm older now, I have produced champions, achieved my goals, and I am interested in other things. I spend time with my *sempai*, my senior students, the ones who have been with me for many years. Now, I'm not interested in champions; I'm interested in teachers. But this will change too. I can only tell you what I live today, what I believe right now. Everything is a phase. We say in Japan you are always a beginner— even when you die, it is for the first time. There is never a final word. Only this moment.

While technique is of course important, I no longer promote my students according to their ability. To me, only time and dedication count. Not everyone is a natural. Someone who struggles and works hard—they have let karate sink into them. When they need it that one time in life, it will be there. They

have *zanchin* because they have fought so hard to learn. The "natural" athletes who learn movements easily are much worse off. They look good—like a mannequin—but when they need to use what they have learned, it won't be there. This is hard for my senior students to accept. They think the karate must look good to get a promotion. It is a mistake. I have seen the best karate. All that really matters is what kind of human being you are.

Visualization is the most important thing. The mind must make the movements first. See what it is you want to do, then the body is free to execute. If the intention is not in the mind first, the technique will be weak, confused. You must do the motion perfectly in your mind. Then release the body, just let it go. This is almost lost today.

Sport karate has turned the art into a pretty dance. There is no substance, nothing meaningful left, just a hollow shell. *Ikken hisatsu*—one punch kills—is the essence of karate. Put everything—your whole life—into one punch. Make the movement perfect, from the inside. This is the idea behind seppuku, ritual suicide, in Japan. You cut open your belly to redeem yourself, to show you are clean inside. That is karate. Be a good person. Be strong. Do what you do with your whole life.

Today, students race to learn every *kata*. We would spend five years on one *kata*, then move to the next. When people ask me now about them, I have no answers. I learned all the *kata*, but then I gave them away. I gave them to my students. I am free of them. They must find the feeling for themselves.

Everything is about feeling. About feeling in your stomach. About intensity. Without feeling, there is no karate. Without commitment to the motions, there is nothing. People who only learn the mechanics are just exercising, there is no martial art in what they do. It is nothing unless you risk everything—unless the feeling that you might die is present in every motion. For this, there are no shortcuts.

Many students ask me to teach them more advanced *kata*— they always want to know the most complicated ones. It's ridiculous. They can hardly do the simple *kata*. How can they hope to move to more advanced movements when they're still having trouble with the basics? It was never like that in Japan. No one did the fancy *katas* everyone uses for competition today. We were never taught them. Actually, we were never taught anything directly. We had to learn everything by watching the students with the best form and by finding ways to mimic them. That was all

> It is nothing unless you risk everything—unless the feeling that you might die is present in every motion.

there was to it: Pick up what you can by watching other people and by experimenting on your own.

You must have passion for practicing. You must want to practice, must have spirit. This is something the instructor cannot give, cannot teach. Spirit and passion must come from within the self. You can be taught various techniques, but if it's a carbon copy with no feeling, no intensity, it's a worthless movement. For students, passion is what is most important. For teachers, compassion.

Good teachers are understanding. They are stern, rough, tough when they need to be, but at the same time give students a pat on the back, tell them it will be okay. You beat the hell out of them one day, and the next you tell them that they did all right, that they're improving.

The instructor's duty is to find the student's good points and to develop them to the best of their ability instead of trying to teach something the student isn't good at. For instance, a student may not be able to kick because of bad knees. A poor instructor will teach the kick regardless, because of some narrow idea about karate, and so will spend more time teaching kicking than on developing the student's good points. On the other hand, a good instructor will develop the student's strong points first, to a level he's happy with, then go back to incorporate kicking. Just because

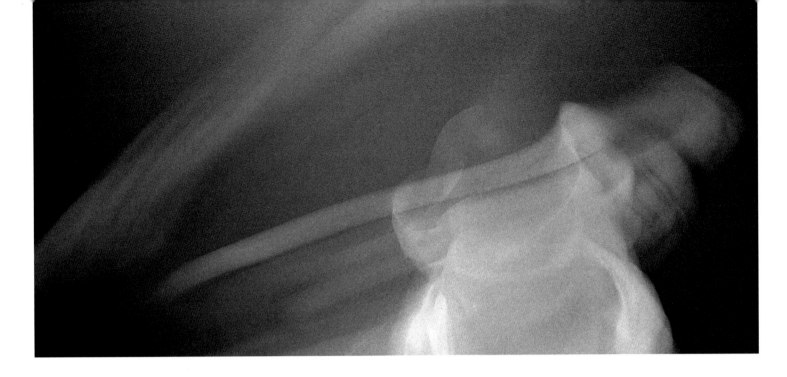

there's a side kick in the *kata*, it doesn't mean a front kick can't be substituted instead, or a lunge punch. If you can't kick, don't kick—that's my philosophy. I mean, if the student is five or six years old, fine, we can force them to learn any technique. But when a person is thirty, forty or fifty years old, it's not always so simple. You can mold a five-year-old kid like plasticine. But when they're thirty or forty, the mold has already been set. You'd have to break everything apart to build something new.

Don't forget that the essence of karate can be traced back two thousand years, and its movements have been modified in many ways as it has migrated around the globe. For instance, changes occurred when karate moved from China to Okinawa. The Okinawans were a conquered people and needed to defend

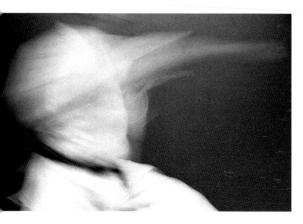

themselves. They didn't have time to learn esoteric movements, so they adopted short stances and sharp, practical techniques. When karate moved from Okinawa to Japan, the focus was placed on physical development, so the movements became bigger. When karate spread from Japan to North America, the sport aspect was emphasized. With each change, the best parts of technique and philosophy have been kept, but little by little the original form has been lost.

This isn't necessarily a bad thing. We don't live in the age of the Model T anymore. I live in this environment, and I teach my students how to survive here and now. Maybe in fifty years, all the techniques I'm teaching now will be a little varied—I can't predict that. But the basic body structure of people and the way we move will not change. And that's all I worry about: teaching how to use the body well.

You should consider your body as a spring. The tighter you coil its center, the faster, the more powerful it gets. You have to load up the body to move explosively. People have a tendency, though, of developing upper-body muscle and leaving their lower body, where they have to stand, weak. When you're young, you just use brute strength anyway and can get away with it. But as you grow older, you need to develop more efficiency, to cut out unnecessary movement. So you try to find ways not to waste energy.

I always suggest to people around twenty-five or thirty that they start teaching little kids. You learn patience, of course, but it also forces you to visualize someone else's movement. It makes you think of different approaches, about how you might teach a movement to someone with a different body type than your own, and in the process you begin to learn your own anatomy that much more. When you find a student's weak area, you have to go out and develop a method of helping him. You can't borrow an exercise from somebody else—there's no thought behind using somebody else's technique.

Many teachers, like myself when I was younger, start out wanting to produce champions and forget everything else to concentrate on that. But if you've got a hundred students, only one can be the champion. Maybe ten altogether will compete, so that means that ninety of them are not involved. So you're spending all your time and energy on these ten people at the expense of all the others. Champions have natural ability or else they wouldn't be champions. They have talent, they're eager; they'll dig up the ability to win from somewhere and become champions regardless of what you teach them. Teachers think they develop champions, but the truth is, champions develop themselves. Teachers just want to take credit for it. That's human nature, I suppose.

Inner power can only be developed through practice. You might understand the theory, but to make it practical is very difficult. You've got to practice, practice, practice. It's natural for you to forget how to use the body in just the right way. So every time you practice, it might take your body an hour to remember a technique properly. But in another two weeks, maybe that time is shortened to forty-five minutes. Over time, your body remembers things more quickly, and so all of a sudden you're doing the technique correctly without even knowing it.

With inner power, the tendency is to start to move your strength from the center of your body up to your shoulders, which is incorrect. When you realize this during practice and force yourself to overcome this, you might last five seconds—but at least you remembered what was important. So the next time you do an hour practice, instead of five seconds, you might remember for ten seconds, then one minute, two minutes, three minutes, and gradually you acquire the motion. Then you find out, when someone asks you to teach them what you have learned, that you can't, because you yourself don't know how or when you got it right. You try and then you forget, you try and then you forget, over and over—that's the pattern. But eventually, instead of forgetting, you start remembering.

Let's say during practice you do a thousand kicks on each leg.

You might ask yourself what the hell the point is. It only takes one kick to kill a person, so why bother? But then, later on, your leg comes out without thinking about it. You're kicking. Through continuous practice, it comes. Then you realize the kick is there, but the technique is not, so you go on to the next stage. A lot of people try to polish the technique first, before they even acquire it.

Teachers think they develop champions, but the truth is, champions develop themselves.

In judo, we grab, we throw, we choke—there's a satisfaction in that. But in karate, we often have false ideas about our techniques. We think, because we learn a karate punch, the person is supposed to die when they're hit. But you punch me and I don't feel it. You think to yourself, "I've been punching for fifteen years and I can't even hurt a guy. There must be something I'm doing wrong." The damage wasn't nearly what it was supposed to be. The interpretation was false.

When you break a brick, there's a wrong way and there's a right way. When you know the difference and you can do it, you build confidence. You've got to develop your body to accept pain. Let's say you go out and hit the *makiwara*. Next day, your hand is

puffed up, black and blue. Are you going to go and give it soft little taps because it hurts? Or are you going to wait six months until it heals and then swell it right back up on the first punch? No. Grit your teeth. Punch. It hurts, it hurts, it hurts, it hurts— after a while, your hand goes numb. So you learn patience, a tolerance of pain and to not give up. That's karate. Pain is temporary. Death is permanent.

All of the martial arts understand this. All of them put the body through rigors. It is not enough to say you have a modest heart. You must have it under the most excruciating circumstances, so that a true benevolence develops. You have to "eat the raw rice." Train hard and train with greater ideals in mind. That is the Way.

All of the martial arts are in continuous development. There will always be some master, some supernatural master, in Canada, in Japan, wherever, that will carry on. It's not restricted to the Japanese—many Western people have reached the goal already. But they've done so very quietly. They don't go out and exploit themselves. There are quite a few of them, practicing on their own. Occasionally a young fifteen-year-old kid will become a champion. They crop up periodically. If they continue, they will become the next grand master. But if they become big-headed, by eighteen they'll be spoiled and won't carry on because success came too easily for them.

When I was younger and I went to the dojo, there was a guy there. I thought he was fifty, but when you're fifteen, everybody over thirty looks like an old guy. Anyway, he used to practice by himself. He had very good technique, very sharp, but he would never fight with me when I asked him. He would just say, "No, thank you. I'm just practicing by myself. I'll watch you fight. You go ahead." So I thought he was chicken—he would never fight. Well, one day I got drunk and I got very vulgar with him. He looked at me and said, "That's not the Way. I must fix you."

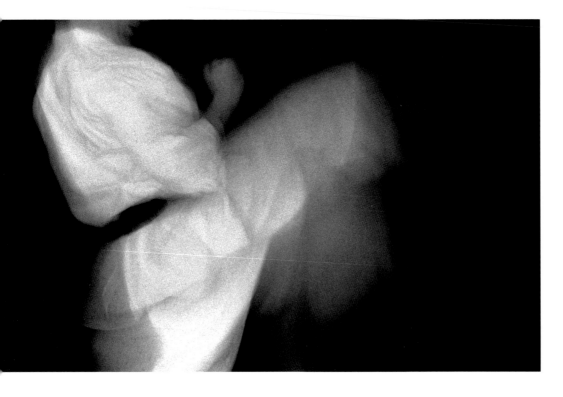

And—bam!—that was it. It didn't take him two seconds. I woke up on my back. These are the type of people—that are very quiet, that don't have to go out and show what they can do—that I am talking about. They practice to better themselves. That's their philosophy. And they don't have to prove anything in the process.

When I started, it was right after the war and the country was in a mess. There was no law, and naturally the fittest survived. I saw a lot of people get beat up, and I experienced that myself. I said to myself that nobody was ever going to do that to me again. So my determination in the beginning was self-defense. But then, as you train, you develop confidence, and then you don't have to fight to prove you're tougher than the other guy. That was the change for me, anyway, and I think it's probably the same for other people too.

I've been very fortunate with the students I've had. I've been able to share many aspects of life with them and develop a strong sense of camaraderie. It's the life I love, you know, karate. Not for the money, but to be able to train and teach and be happy. A lot of people say I'm not a businessman, which I'm not, and I don't care. As long as I can eat tomorrow and be happy, that's all that matters. What am I going to do with a million dollars? Who cares what I spend it on if I'm not happy? My focus now is on the younger generation, on preparing them for a life in karate. That's what makes me happy.

It's the parents' responsibility to provide moral education to children. Martial arts just reinforce the ideals of society. The point is to be able to hold your head high and walk without having to look behind you. Have nothing to hide, have nothing to be scared of facing up to—that's what we have to teach kids. Honesty. To be honest.

Learning the proper way is not impossible. People talk too much! One student will talk about a technique for five years and learn nothing. Another will practice for five years and master it. There is no secret. Practice, practice. I still practice, I'm still looking to improve. If people think they've got it, they've figured it out, they might as well die. You have to always be searching. If you think you've mastered it, that may as well be the end of your life, because you've got no more will, nothing to look for. You've got to keep on searching for something. You have to always be a beginner.

The Disciplines

AIKIDO

Translates literally as "the way of harmony with the universal force." The name was adopted formally in 1942 to describe the martial art founded by Morihei Ueshiba. The techniques of aikido, influenced by Ueshiba's mastery of the spear and sword, as well as unarmed combat, are characterized by flowing, circular throws and joint locks. A deeply philosophical art, aikido seeks to develop harmony with nature by uniting the life force of the individual with the life force, or *ki*, of the universe.

ATARASHII NAGINATA

The name "new naginata" was adopted after World War II to describe the unified practice of the sportive art of naginata formed from several *koryu* (old flow; nomenclature for ancient styles, schools or traditions), including Tendo-Ryu and Jikishinkage-Ryu. Although it is unclear precisely when naginata was first developed (early contact with the Chinese may have inspired it), its curved-blade staff became a popular weapon of war with the samurai of the Heian Period (794–1190). The naginata is wielded with large sweeping motions combining the dynamics of the staff, saber and spear. Earlier incarnations of this style of weapon, called *nagamaki*, had longer *ha* (blades) than *e* (hafts)—the reverse proportion of naginata. During the Edo Period (1603–1867) the naginata ceased to be used on the battlefield and was regarded as a defensive weapon for women of samurai families. In the following Meiji Period (1868–1912) naginata was seen as a women's martial art, used to promote physical strength and the virtues of order, harmony, chastity and moderation. The Zen Nihon Naginata Renmei (All Japan Naginata Federation) was formed in 1955 and authorized by Japan's Ministry of Education in 1968. In 1990, the International Naginata Federation was founded. Today, men as well as women from around the globe practice atarashii naginata's two main elements of *kata*, using wood naginata (among advanced practitioners), and *jigeiko/shiai* (practice sparring/contest), using naginata made of wood and bamboo. The use of metal-bladed naginata is very rare today.

IAIDO

The founding of "the way of drawing the sword" is commonly attributed to Jinsuke Hayashizaki, who is believed to have lived between 1546 and 1621. According to legend, the art was conceived by Jinsuke as the result of divine inspiration, after he had prayed and practiced austerely with his sword at Hayashizaki Myojin shrine in Okura village (in modern Yamagata prefecture) for 100 days. Jinsuke is known to have studied swordsmanship for seven years, between 1595 and 1601, before creating a method of sword-drawing he called *battojutsu* (striking sword technique), which inspired the creation of some 200 schools during his lifetime. Primarily a solo practice, iaido is the art of drawing a sword and cutting with it in the same motion. Iaido practitioners follow a typical pattern of drawing (*nukitsuke*) and cutting (*kiritsuke*), delivering a finishing cut (*kirikudashi*), and then cleaning the blade (*chiburi*) and returning it to the scabbard (*noto*), while keeping eyes fixed on an imaginary opponent. The Zen Nihon Iaido Renmei (All Japan Iaido Federation), an umbrella organization of several branches of iaido, was formed in 1948. The larger Zen Nihon Kendo Renmei (All Japan Kendo Federation), however, formed a committee to develop a standardized iaido curriculum to revive and strengthen kendo's historical connection to the sword in 1967. The twelve forms compiled by the Zen Nihon Kendo Renmei are the most widely practiced iaido forms in the world, and are considered a "primer" for more specialized iaido study.

JUDO

More precisely called Kodokan judo, this art known as "the gentle way" was founded in 1882 by Professor Jigoro Kano. Kodokan judo incorporates the strengths of various jujutsu styles, principally Kito-Ryu and Tenshin Shinyo-Ryu, while eliminating their more dangerous techniques. A highly educated man, Kano placed great emphasis on judo as a tool for physical education and moral and intellectual training. Judo's popularity increased dramatically following a famous contest hosted by the Tokyo Metropolitan Police Board in 1886, between fifteen practitioners of Kodokan judo and fifteen members of a leading jujutsu school of the time. The result of thirteen wins for the Kodokan and two draws firmly established Kodokan judo's supremacy over jujutsu in the public's eyes. While the technical aspects of Kodokan judo were finalized around 1887, its spiritual expression realized full form in 1922, when the Kodokan Bunkakai (Kodokan Cultural Society) was established under the banner of judo's famous slogans *seiryoku zenyo* (maximum efficiency) and *jita kyoei* (perfection of self, and mutual welfare and benefit). In 1964 men's judo—the first Asian art to become a medal sport—became a part of Olympic competition at the Tokyo Summer Games. In 1992 judo competition for women was added to the Olympics in Barcelona.

KARATE-DO

The "way of the empty hand" was originally known as *toudi*, or "Chinese hand," in reference to the influence Chinese boxing had on this martial art during its formation on the island of Okinawa. The Okinawans of prehistory had improvised their own rudimentary form of hand-to-hand self-defense, and were later influenced by the Japanese fighting traditions of the Heian Period through the immigration of Japanese aristocrats. The first systematic transmission of Chinese fighting traditions to Okinawa is believed to trace to the "Thirty-Six Families." This group of Chinese immigrants established a trade mission in Kume village in 1393, where, over a period of five centuries, Okinawan nobles learned the language, arts and crafts of the residing—and visiting—Chinese diplomats. In 1507 King Sho Shin banned privately owned weapons when the "Act of Eleven Distinctions" was ratified, ending feudalism in the Ryukyu Kingdom and precipitating a new era in Okinawa's cultivation of unarmed self-defense. In February 1609, Yoshihisa Shimazu, the head of the Satsuma clan, invaded the Ryukyu Kingdom and initiated Japan's 270-year military occupation of Okinawa, which saw the disarmament of the Okinawan people extend to government personnel, and the flourishing of *kobudo* (weapons-based martial arts), using farming implements. The *pechin*, mid-ranked Okinawan officials who were the main purveyors of Okinawan combat systems, traveled to Satsuma throughout the occupation and learned the fighting principles of the Satsuma samurai, further affecting the maturation of Okinawa's fighting traditions. Although there is evidence of earlier pioneers, Gichin Funakoshi is credited with the official introduction of karate-jutsu (Chinese hand technique) to Japan. While earlier demonstrations of the art had taken place both in Okinawa and Japan, on March 6, 1921, Japan's Crown Prince Hirohito visited Okinawa while en route to Europe and witnessed a karate-jutsu demonstration put on by Funakoshi. He issued a formal invitation to the Okinawan Shobukai (Martial Spirit Promotion Society), headed by Funakoshi, to participate in Japan's first National Athletic Exhibition in the early spring of 1922. Karate-jutsu flourished in Japan following the demonstration, and Funakoshi never returned to his home in Okinawa, choosing instead to teach karate in Japan, first to employees of private companies and then at various Japanese universities. The two original ideograms for karate, meaning "China hand," can be pronounced either as *karate* or *toudi*. In December of 1933, the prestigious Dai Nippon Butokukai (All Japan Martial Arts Federation) ratified a change of the first ideogram to an alternate reading of *kara*, meaning "empty," thus removing the Chinese reference. A *do* suffix has replaced *jutsu*, signifying karate-do's acceptance as a form of Japanese *budo*.

KENDO

The "way of the sword" has a long history in Japan. Although Chinese swords first appeared in the second century BC, it wasn't until the Nara Period (710–794) that the *katana*, the distinctive single-edged, curved Japanese sword, emerged. Great strides in the swordsmith's art occurred during the Kamakura Period (1185–1333), and in the Muromachi Period (1392–1573) the techniques of *kenjutsu* (ancient sword method) began to be systematized. During the sixteenth and seventeenth centuries, the philosophical and spiritual underpinnings of Japanese swordsmanship were influenced by Ittosai Ito, the founder of Itto-Ryu (One Sword Style); Ise-no-kami Kozumi, the founder of Shin Kage-Ryu (New Shadow Style); and Musashi Miyamoto, the famous author of the *Go Rin No Sho* (*The Book of Five Rings*) and founder of Hyo Ho Niten Ichi Ryu (Two Heavens as One School of Strategy). Kendo began to emphasize spiritual development. For safety reasons, *bogu* (kendo armor) was introduced and the sword was replaced with a *shinai*. This new form of sword play promoted a more active and competitive style of practice whose appeal reached beyond the samurai class. In 1871, kendo began to be practiced in Japan's first modern civic police force. And in 1905, Tokyo University became the first college in the nation to sponsor a kendo team. 1928 saw the establishment of the Zen Nihon Kendo Renmei (All Japan Kendo Federation), although it would be disbanded in 1946 due to the prohibition on martial art practice instituted by the occupying Allied forces. It was re-established on October 14, 1952, and authorized as a foundation on February 22, 1972.

KYUDO

The origins of "the way of the bow" date back to Japan's earliest primitive people, the Jomon, a Mesolithic culture who thrived from the eleventh century to the third century BC, and who are known to have hunted with short, symmetrical bows. Around the third century BC, the Jomon were displaced by a wave of immigrants from northern China, known as the Yayoi, who introduced agriculture, bronze work and the religious practices that would eventually develop into Shinto. During this period, it is believed that the unique asymmetrical design of the Japanese bow, whose grip is located approximately one third of the way up the bow's length, emerged. The unique aesthetic of the Japanese bow is a reflection of its status as an object of veneration and a symbol of political power. The legendary Emperor Jinmu, said to have founded the Japanese Imperial line, is always depicted with bow in hand. By the tenth century AD, Japanese bow makers had adopted the Chinese construction of composite bows, using wood and bamboo. In 1192, shogun (military governor) Yoritomo Minamoto instructed Nagakiyo Ogasawara, the founder of Ogasawara-Ryu, to teach formalized horse-mounted archery. Another influential archer was Masatsugu Danjo Heki, who is credited with assuring the continued growth of Japanese archery by standardizing the training of kyujutsu (archery technique). The latter portion of the Warring States Period (1477–1573) saw the construction of the bow reach its pinnacle, just as its usefulness as a weapon of war disappeared with the introduction of muskets by the Portugese in 1543. Kyudo might not have survived into the twenty-first century if not for Toshizane Honda (1836–1917), who combined elements of the warrior styles of the samurai and the ceremonial styles of the Imperial court nobles to create a hybrid known as Honda-Ryu, which, despite resistance from traditional schools, found acceptance with the public. In order to promote growth, modern kyudo was standardized in 1949, when the Zen Nihon Kyudo Renmei (All Japan Kyudo Federation [AJKF]) was formed. In 1953, the AJKF published the *Kyudo Kyohan* (*Kyudo Manual*) establishing standards of shooting form and practice.

SHORINJI KEMPO

"The Way of the Shaolin Temple Fist" was founded in 1947 on the island of Shikoku by Doshin So (1911–1980), known to the followers of Shorinji Kempo simply as *Kaiso*, or founder. More than a martial art, Shorinji Kempo is also a registered religious organization, whose members practice Kongo Zen, a form of Zen Buddhism. Doshin So, who worked for Japan's Special Service Agency in Manchuria during the Second World War, trained widely in Chinese martial arts, eventually becoming a Grand Master and the successor to the Northern Shorinji Giwamonken Kempo school. Deeply influenced by the devastation and lawlessness he witnessed during and after the war, Doshin So resolved to aid the defeated Japanese people in restoring their pride. After dreaming of the Zen saint Dharuma-daishi, he combined his experience in Shaolin boxing with a philosophical imperative of self-reliance to form what is now Shorinji Kempo. The martial art separates techniques into two classes: the kicks and punches of *goho* (hard method), and the joint manipulations and throws of *juho* (soft method). In addition, *seiho* (healing method) is used to promote health and muscle relaxation through massage and acupressure.

Glossary

age uke: rising block

ai: love; harmony

azuchi: name of the target bank in Japanese archery

bogu: kendo armor

budo: The literal translation, "martial ways," is used often—including in this text—to refer to *gendai budo*, or the modern martial ways of Japan. *Gendai budo* are martial arts that became finalized after the Meiji restoration of 1868. Martial arts in existence prior to 1868 are referred to as *bujutsu*, martial methods, or more specifically *koryu bujutsu*, old tradition, or ancient martial methods. The *do* suffix, which means path or way, denotes the spiritual emphasis of modern martial arts and their implicit ideals of character building, as opposed to the more combat-oriented *koryu* traditions.

chambara: slang for Japanese swashbuckler films that chronicle the exploits of feudal-era samurai

dai-hanshi: great master, a formal title

dan: black belt level

do: chest; also the Way, the path

dojo: place of the Way; training hall

fudoshin: immoveable mind; imperturbability

Funakoshi sensei: Gichin Funakoshi (1868–1957) is commonly regarded as "the father of modern karate" and is the author of five early books on the subject. Born in Shuri, Okinawa, Funakoshi began his study of *toudi* (Chinese hand, later known as karate) at the age of eleven, initially to combat his frail health, under masters Yasutsune Azato and Yasutsune

Itosu. At age twenty-one, he became an elementary school teacher, and in 1922 he gave the first formal demonstration of karate in mainland Japan at the first National Athletic Exhibition. In May 1948, Funakoshi—at age eighty-one—was named chief instructor emeritus of the newly organized Nihon Karate Kyokai (Japan Karate Association). Gichin Funakoshi died on April 26, 1957. (See also **Shotokan**.)

hanshi: master, a formal title usually bestowed at eighth-degree black belt

hara: abdomen; stomach

Higaonna sensei: Morio Higaonna (1938–) is the chief instructor and founder of the International Okinawan Goju-Ryu Karate-do Federation (IOGKF), which now has approximately 50,000 members in forty-five member countries. One of the world's most respected karate instructors, he began training at the age of fourteen in Okinawa, Japan. Higaonna sensei currently holds the rank of ninth-degree black belt.

ichigo ichi e: The phrase "one time, one meeting" first appeared in *Yamanoue Soji Ki* (*The Record of Yamanoue Soji*). The phrase, which expresses the uniqueness of each moment and the importance of appreciating every encounter, was rediscovered and popularized by the *daimyo* (feudal lord) and tea master Ii Naosuke (1815–1860) in his book *Chanoyu Ichie Shu* (*Mannerisms in the Tea Ceremony*). Although originally associated with the tea ceremony, the concept of the unrepeatable and transient nature of experience is widespread in Japanese culture. *Ikebana* (flower arranging), *shodo* (the way of calligraphy) and *budo* (martial ways) all exemplify the importance of seizing the moment without error.

iki-ai: how to breathe

ikken hissastu: The maxim "to kill with one blow," popular among karate-do adherents, represents the need for decisiveness and commitment in an attack. The idea is represented in karate's ippon (one-point) principle, in which contests are decided by a single strike.

inga oho: literally "karma" and "retribution"

inochi gake: put your life on the line; literally "life" and "cliff"

ippon: one full point in competition

jita kyoei: The ideal of "perfection of self, and mutual welfare and benefit" is one of the two popular mottos of Kodokan judo (see also **seiryoku zenyo**) established by Jigoro Kano (see **Kano sensei**). The perfection of self was to be undertaken altruistically, in order to be of service to the larger community. Kano described "welfare and benefit" as a condition of physical health with well-developed intellect and morals and the ability to appreciate beauty. The true search for "welfare and benefit," in Kano's view, includes a desire for others to also prosper. In this way, Kano asserted, the ultimate object of judo is the ultimate object of humankind.

jodan zuki: high punch

ju: flexible, pliable, submissive, harmonious, adaptable, yielding

judo-ka: judo practitioner

jujutsu: the practice of flexibility; a generic term for a variety of systems of fighting while minimally armed; the ancient precursor to modern judo

Kano sensei: The founder of judo, Jigoro Kano (1860–1938) studied under Hachinosuke Fukuda and Masatomo Iso, both of the Tenshin Shinyo-Ryu, and Tsunetoshi Iikubo of the Kito-Ryu, receiving initiation into the secrets of both schools. In 1882 he established the Kodokan and began teaching Kodokan judo. In 1909, when Japan received an invitation to participate in the International Olympic Committee (IOC), Kano was chosen as Japan's first IOC representative. He became the first president of the Japan Amateur Athletic Association in 1911. Jigoro Kano died on May 4, 1938, returning to Japan from an IOC meeting in Cairo, where he had succeeded in nominating Tokyo as the host of the 1940 Olympics, which were to include judo as an Olympic sport for the first time. (The Games were later cancelled due to the outbreak of the Second World War.)

kata: forms; ritualized patterns

katana: long sword

keichu: concentration

keien: walk

keiko: practice

ken: sword

kendo-ka: kendo practitioner

ki: energy; life force

kibadachi: horse-riding stance

kime: focus

Kodokan: Literally "the hall for studying the Way," the Kodokan (formally the Kodokan International Judo Center) is the headquarters of Kodokan judo. Located in Tokyo, the current eight-story building was dedicated in 1984 to commemorate the hundredth anniversary of the adoption of the Kodokan's bylaws, and the formal adoption of the name Kodokan judo.

koenkai: support group

kote: wrist/forearm

kote-zuki: wrist-thrust combination in kendo

ku: emptiness

kumite: sparring, fighting

kun: maxims

kyoshi: master teacher, a formal title usually bestowed at seventh-degree black belt

kyujutsu: the technique of archery; the ancient precursor to kyudo

makiwara: rolled up straw; the name given to a striking board, wrapped in straw, used in traditional karate training

men: head

mushin: no mind; not thinking; without conscience

nanikuso: spirit

nidan: second degree black belt

Ohtsuka sensei: Hironori Ohtsuka (1892–1982), the founder of Wado-Ryu karate, began training in jujutsu in 1898 under the tutelage of his great uncle. In 1905, Ohtsuka began the study of Shindo Yoshin-Ryu jujutsu under the third Grand Master of the style, Tatsusaburo Nakayama. In 1920 he was awarded *Menkyo-Kaiden*, designating his full proficiency in Shindo Yoshin-Ryu, and licensing him as fourth Grand Master of the style. In 1934 Ohtsuka published rules for *yakusoku kumite*, or non-contact free sparring, and laid the foundation for modern sport karate. Ohtsuka created the name Wado-Ryu to represent his synthesis of karate and jujutsu. In 1941, he received *kyoshi* (master teacher) licenses, and in 1966, Emperor Hirohito awarded Ohtsuka the Fifth Order of Merit of the Sacred Treasure (the Cordon of the Rising Sun) for his contributions to karate. Ohtsuka was presented with the title Shodai Karate-do Meijin Judan (first generation karate master of the tenth dan) by the Kokusai Budo Renmei (International Martial Arts Federation) in 1972, the first such honor bestowed upon a karate master.

okagesama: because of you; your assistance

randori: free-style practice

-Ryu: -style

sandan: third-degree black belt

seiryoku zenyo: "Maximum efficiency," one of the two popular mottos of Kodokan judo (see also **jita kyoei**) espoused by judo's founder, Jigoro Kano (see **Kano sensei**). It refers to the most judicious employment of energy—both mental and physical. While "maximum efficiency" is sought in judo's techniques of *kuzushi* (unbalancing the opponent), *tsukuri* (positioning to prepare to throw the opponent) and *kake* (throwing), it is also the goal of daily living, to be attained through the conformity of spiritual and physical strength. This larger goal of judo prompted Kano to establish the Kodokan Bunkakai (Kodokan Cultural Association) in 1922, with the aim of improving the larger sphere of human endeavor (*seiryoku zenyo* is often also translated as "worthy use of human efforts"), including the building of personal health, national unity, societal harmony and human prosperity. The best application of the concept of "maximum efficiency," Kano believed, is to one's own self-realization. But Kano also believed that self-realization is attained through the mutual realization of others. Together, *seiryoku zenyo* and *jita kyoei*, present a unified basis for the pursuit of human prosperity.

seishin: meditation course

seiza: seated position; used to refer to seated meditation

sempai: senior student

sen: teach

sensei: a generic term for teacher; literally "one who has gone before"

seppuku: ritual suicide by disembowelment

shiai: competition; match; bout

shihan: great expert

shinai: split-bamboo Japanese fencing weapon

shinan: instruction; pointing south

Shinto: "The way of the Gods" is the indigenous national religion of Japan. It dates back to at least the middle of the first millennium BC. The early folk religion became systematized to differentiate itself from other religions when Buddhism reached Japan in either 538 or 552 AD. Unlike many religions, Shinto has no founder, no written scriptures, no congregational worship and no explicitly stated religious law or moral code, yet it deeply influences the psyche, values and motivations of the Japanese people. Its practice is largely connected to the ritual worshipping of deities and to *matsuri*, festivals celebrating the cycles of nature. Essentially animistic, Shinto perceives a spiritual essence within both animate and inanimate aspects of nature.

shodan: first-degree black belt

Shotokan: *Shoto* was the pen name of Gichin Funakoshi (see **Funakoshi sensei**). It is formed from the words "pine tree" and "wave," and was taken from Funakoshi's boyhood memory of the sound of wind passing through pine trees in the hills of Shuri. *Kan* means building or hall. After the building of Funakoshi's first karate dojo, his students named it the Shotokan, or "the house of Shoto." The inauguration for the dojo was held on July 29, 1939. However, the Shotokan was destroyed on March 10, 1945, during the Tokyo fire bombings. Over time, the name Shotokan became associated with Funakoshi's style of karate—one of the most widely practiced styles in the world today.

shu ha ri: The axiom "protect, diverge, separate" describes three broad and often overlapping phases of progression encountered on the journey from novice to master level. *Shu* refers to a thorough absorption of the basics of an art, to faithfulness to one's teacher and to maintaining tradition. *Ha* is the process of breaking free of tradition and the emergence of the student's individuality. It is also a stage of introspection, in which the physical demands of the previous stage are informed by inward discovery. *Ri* is the final stage of transition, marking the student's assimilation of the art and ability to offer a unique interpretation. Beyond simple independence, this highest level, attained through a lifetime of study and the complete internalization of the art, marks the student's breakthrough to enlightenment.

sumo: Traditional Japanese wrestling; the national sport of Japan. The prehistoric origins of sumo served religious purposes associated with Shinto harvest rituals. The earliest written record of sumo, found in the *Kojiki* (*Record of Ancient Matters*), tells of a grappling contest between the gods Takemikazuchi no Kami and Takeminakata no Kumi. Takemikazuchi no Kami, from whom the Japanese Imperial family is said to descend, won the contest and secured control of the Japanese archipelago for the Japanese people. Early formalized techniques and regulations of sumo were introduced during the Nara Period (710–794), following sumo's inclusion in the ceremonies of the Imperial Court. During the military rule of the Kamakura Period (1185–1333), sumo was pursued chiefly as a martial art. The peaceful and prosperous Edo Period (1603–1867) saw sumo's popularization as a form of entertainment for the emerging middle class, the patronage of sumo players from various *daimyo* (Japanese feudal lords), and the first sumo match to observe standardized rules and ring specifications. The modern term for a sumo wrestler, *rikishi*, meaning "strong warrior," emerged in the early eighteenth century.

suzumushi: bell insect, a species of singing cricket

Tannisho: *Lamentation on Deviations*, one of the most widely read works in Japanese Buddhism, is regarded as both a religious and a literary classic. The work contains the sayings of Shinran (1173–1263), the founder of Jodo Shinshu (Pure Land) Buddhism, as remembered several decades after Shinran's death by his close disciple Yui-en.

tatami: Japanese straw floor covering

Tempu sensei: Tempu Nakamura (1876–1969) was an acquaintance of Morihei Ueshiba (see **Ueshiba sensei**) who created a self-improvement system called Shin Shin Toitsu Do. The concepts and exercises of the system, based on elements of yoga and the martial arts, influenced several notable aikido practitioners.

Tenshin Koryu Bo-Jutsu: a classical school of Japanese stick fighting

tokonoma: a recessed alcove in a traditional Japanese home, usually decorated with artwork

tsuki: thrust

uchideshi: live-in student; special disciple; apprentice

ukemi: breakfall; literally "fall"

Ueshiba sensei: Morihei Ueshiba (1883–1969), the founder of aikido, began his career in the martial arts in 1901, when he studied Tenshin Shinyo-Ryu jujutsu (one of the main influences on Kodokan judo) under Tokusaburo Tozawa. In 1903, about the same time he joined the Sixty-First Army Infantry Regiment, Ueshiba began a five-year study of Goto-Ha Yagyu Shingan-Ryu (a school of weapons and jujutsu techniques). He was sent to the Manchurian Front to fight in the Russo-Japanese War in 1905, and was discharged from the army in 1906. Ueshiba next studied judo under Kiyoichi Takagi, after returning to his home in Tanabe. In 1912 Ueshiba met and began to train with Sokaku Takeda, a teacher of Daito-Ryu jujutsu (a Meiji Period school of jujutsu). Takeda had a great impact on Ueshiba's creation of *aiki budo*—the precursor to aikido. In December 1919 Ueshiba met Onisaburo Deguchi, a reverend in the Omoto religion (a sect of Shinto), beginning a relationship that was to deeply influence Ueshiba's spirituality. He moved to Ayabe, the spiritual center of the Omoto sect, where he opened his first dojo, the Ueshiba Juku (Ueshiba Private School) in 1921. Three years later, Ueshiba accompanied Deguchi on an ill-fated trip to establish a utopian religious colony in Manchuria. The members of the party were arrested by Chinese authorities and threatened with execution, but were spared at the last moment when Japanese authorities intervened on their behalf. Ueshiba moved to Tokyo in 1927, and established the Kobukan Dojo, a large, eighty-mat school of 200 members, including powerful military admirals, in 1931. In May 1937 Ueshiba began regular study of Kashima Shinto-Ryu (a 500-year-old weapons-based martial art). In 1942 Ueshiba retired to Iwama, in Ibaraki Prefecture, after resigning from his teaching posts in Tokyo (several of which were military academies) in protest of the war. A year later, he built Aiki Shrine, an Omoto shrine that symbolized his belief in aikido's spiritual essence. It was during his time in Iwama, spent farming and operating his new dojo (the *hombu dojo* [head school] of the Aikikai Foundation), that Ueshiba is said to have perfected aikido. In 1960 Ueshiba received the *Shiju Hosho* (Purple Ribbon Medal of Honor) from the Japanese government. A new (and still the current) *hombu dojo* was dedicated in Tokyo's Shinjuku Ward in 1968. On January 15, 1969, Ueshiba gave his final demonstration. He died of liver cancer on April 26, 1969. Morihei Ueshiba's deeply humanistic and spiritual view of the martial arts, as well as accounts of his incredible power, have earned him a reputation as one of history's most acclaimed martial artists.

Wado-Ryu: way of peace; a style of karate, influenced by jujutsu, founded officially in 1938 by Hironori Ohtsuka (see **Ohtsuka sensei**)

waza: technique

zanchin: perfect awareness; remaining spirit

zazen: seated Zen meditation